I0437489

Does Our Money Really Help?

Life in Ethiopia

by

Mike Coote

authorHOUSE®

AuthorHouse™
1663 Liberty Drive, Suite 200
Bloomington, IN 47403
www.authorhouse.com
Phone: 1-800-839-8640

© 2007 Mike Coote. All rights reserved.

No part of this book may be reproduced, stored in a retrieval system, or transmitted by any means without the written permission of the author.

First published by AuthorHouse   9/13/2007

ISBN: 978-1-4343-3772-6 (sc)

Printed in the United States of America
Bloomington, Indiana

This book is printed on acid-free paper.

Acknowledgements

This book has been made possible as a result of CAFOD's invitations to me to visit Ethiopia. I am very grateful to them for the initial inspiration to write it. However the book is entirely my own work and all the views expressed in it are mine.

I am grateful to the local CAFOD staff in Ethiopia – particularly Jannie and Bev for their time, support, encouragement - and logistics! I am also indebted to the two partner organisations – REST and HCS who looked after me so well when 'in the field'. I'd like to count Merid from REST and Belayneh from HCS as new found friends.

Thanks also to the rest of the team from the first trip – Claire, Seb, Paul and Catherine – twenty somethings who made a pensioner feel an equal.

I am also very grateful to Mike Amphlett from 'fixmycommas' for his editing which went far beyond just correcting my spelling and grammar.

I also read a lot about the country. I would particularly recommend:

The Bradt Guide
The Chains of Heaven by Philip Marsden
A History of Ethiopia by Harold G Marcus
and, particularly – *I Didn't Do It For You* by Michela Wrong

And a final thanks to my family for putting up with my verbal diarrhea on my return home!

Contents

Introduction

Africa is perplexing. It is an incredibly beautiful continent and it has many valuable natural resources. Its inhabitants can be charming, conscientious, amusing and selfless. However, there are desperately poor parts of the continent and, despite much help from richer countries over the years, many people still do not have access to the basic levels of food and water necessary for survival.

This conundrum can be exasperating. Is it caused by corrupt governments siphoning off money that was designated to help their populations? Is it that the people have become too dependent on outside help, losing the motivation to help themselves? Is too much money spent on conflict and strife between and within countries rather than on the development of health, education and economic growth? Are the trade rules, as defined by rich countries, harming business development in Africa's poorer nations? These are a few of the many questions we ask of ourselves; they shape attitudes towards the continent and influence the individual's decision as to whether or not to donate money to help.

Although they form a constant backdrop to this book, I shall not attempt to address these macro-level issues; there are many others who are far better placed to be able to offer improvement strategies for the prospects of Africa's large and diverse population in the longer term. However, I do propose to answer the question I am most frequently asked; – *Is it worth giving - does my money really go to help people in need?*

As a former semi-sceptic myself I can now assert that the answer is a very definite 'yes'.

I have chosen to focus upon one African country – Ethiopia – which I have been fortunate to visit twice in recent months. I want to delve deep beneath the macro issues and describe the dramatic changes that have been made to the lives of people and communities by modest amounts of aid from governments and individual donors. I have met people whose lives have been lifted out of a survival struggle to a situation where, by their own efforts, they can build a modest and sustainable income for their families; what is more they can give their children a significantly better start in life than they themselves had. Their stories are in themselves inspiring, but they also enable those in the West who have donated their own money, to feel a little pride in the results that their donations have helped to achieve.

My first visit to Ethiopia was in November 2006 when the aid agency CAFOD (Catholic Agency for Overseas Development) sought volunteers to visit the country for two weeks, primarily to generate media interest in the UK. I wrote a diary of my visit in the book I called 'Ethiopia – A Fleeting Glimpse'. This diary is included here, together with some additional material and updates on what has happened since the visit.

My second visit was in May 2007 when CAFOD invited me to return to help both with the marketing plans for a specific project they had recently initiated and with a 'lessons learnt' review of the project I had visited during the previous November. The book describes my experiences and discusses the impact these projects have had and will continue to have on the lives of some individuals I met.

As a stranger to the developing world, to me these visits were spellbinding, intense, inspiring and humbling. Whatever views one holds on the macro-level issues, there are real people living real lives in Africa. I have witnessed just how much we can help some of them. We have to ensure that, somehow, we provide similar help and opportunity for all the rest.

1

CAFOD –
One of the UK Aid Agencies

CAFOD[1] (Catholic Agency for Overseas Development) is one of a number of Aid Agencies based in the UK. These organisations are in a group often referred to as NGOs (Non-Government Organisations).

CAFOD is the official overseas development and relief agency of the Catholic Church in England and Wales. It is a member of Caritas International[2], a network of similar Catholic organisations around the world. Its mission is to promote human development and social justice. To achieve this it raises funds so that it can work alongside people in need to reduce poverty and bring about sustainable change through development and humanitarian programmes. It also challenges governments and international bodies to adopt policies that promote social justice and end poverty.

CAFOD works with and employs people of all faiths and none, regardless of their race, sex or age. It draws inspiration from Christian scripture, Catholic social teaching and the experiences and hopes of people who are poor, marginalised or oppressed. It makes no attempt whatsoever to persuade or cajole any of its partners or beneficiaries into the Catholic faith.

---

[1] More about CAFOD can be found on their website www.cafod.org.uk

[2] Caritas International is a confederation of 162 Catholic relief, development and social service organisations working to build a better world, especially for the poor and oppressed, in over 200 countries and territories. Caritas works without regard to creed, race, gender, or ethnicity, and is one of the world's largest humanitarian networks. For more see www.caritas.org

CAFOD's work in the third world is done largely through partners; hence it employs relatively fewer staff in-country than some other larger aid agencies. Local staff participation is essential, providing highly valuable insights into the country and managing relationships with partners to ensure effective use of funds. I was fortunate to have been invited to join a conference for CAFOD staff in November 2005 which I found to be a very rewarding experience. Compared to the plethora of business conferences I had attended over the years the CAFOD conference was notable for the enthusiasm, unity of purpose and team sprit amongst the staff. There was little evidence of the personal and political agendas that often influence or even dominate such meetings in the commercial world.

CAFOD spends 82% of its income on delivering its international aid programme. Of the remaining 18%, 9% is spent on education and campaigning, 8% on generating funds and 1% on governance (a polite word for administration and policy-making!). These figures stand up well in comparison with other similar agencies.

Most of the other UK-based Aid Agencies also work in Ethiopia, often in similar ways and on similar projects. I have no reason to doubt that their different approaches and methods will deliver very similar outcomes. So, although the visits were under the auspices of CAFOD, I am sure my observations would apply equally well to Oxfam, Christian Aid, Save the Children, Action Aid, World Vision or any other.

To illustrate the point I reproduce below an extract from Oxfam's website:

[3]*Oxfam's Ethiopia programme is currently shifting its emphasis to working closely through local partners. Working with partners strengthens communities and promotes ways of working with governments. Oxfam's long-term vision of Oxfam in Ethiopia is for:*

All men, women, girls and boys to have better access to food; thus securing their livelihoods and allowing them a greater influence on the decisions affecting their lives.

The programme is increasingly moving to implementation through local partners and Oxfam is building their capacities.

Promoting alternative and non-formal education is a major focus of Oxfam's education aims. The basis of the programme is to engage with

---

[3] *Italic paragraph* from Oxfam's website www.oxfam.org.uk

regional and national governments for improvements in the financing of basic education, particularly investing in girls' education.

Oxfam is working hard to empower communities with the ability and authority to make decisions for themselves and help communities have a voice in government decisions that impact upon them.

The country team is also pushing for better inclusion of citizens in government decisions and supporting the government's efforts in building a vibrant civil society and a nation that is able to hold government and other development actors accountable for their actions.

My perception is that this statement would be equally valid if the word 'OXFAM' was replaced by 'CAFOD'.

You may ask why there are several such organisations with similar activities and whether it might be more efficient for them to amalgamate into a smaller number. In defence of the *status quo* I believe that having discrete organisations each with its own donors and supporters achieves a larger overall financial contribution from the public than would be achieved by fewer Charities. Once 'on the ground' and delivering aid there is far more co-operation between agencies than there is competition; after all, there is more than enough work for everyone.

Some donors to UK Aid Agencies are uncomfortable about their money being spent on education and campaigning, as they believe that their contributions should go directly to poverty relief. I would argue that this expenditure is an investment of donors' money to achieve greater relief of poverty in the future by less direct methods.

CAFOD's education activities are targeted to ensure that future generations are aware of the challenges faced by poorer countries; such that the allocation of their future influence and financial assets is informed by a greater understanding of the world about them. When speaking to students of all ages I am usually considerably encouraged by the sympathetic response I receive. This goes as far as being confronted after a talk by a group of highly motivated young people with some ideas for immediate fund-raising in their school.

On one occasion I was invited back by a group of 10-year olds to judge a CAFOD poster competition they had organised. Having charged entry fees, and bought the prizes out of their own pocket money, they presented me with about £50 of assorted coins from the venture. In CAFOD, education investment includes the production of presentation materials for use in schools, colleges and youth groups. Just as I do, other volunteers use these materials in lectures, talks and classes at no charge other than their travel expenses. Even then many volunteers – including myself - either leave them unclaimed or return them as voluntary donations thus allowing the charity to benefit from Gift Aid). CAFOD staff spend a very small proportion of their time to co-ordinate the work of the volunteers.

Campaigning is aimed at influencing opinion leaders, people in power and particularly governments. CAFOD achieves this by lobbying and by organising positive actions such as demonstrations and vigils; once again much of the actual campaigning activity is conducted by volunteers.

Measuring the impact and value of this investment is not easy now; yet when I think back just a few years our own politicians were so much less likely to accept the need to devote money and effort to assist developing countries. These days, thanks to campaigns like 2005's 'Make Poverty History', to which all the Aid Agencies and many others contributed, the need for the UK Government to play a major role in supporting poorer countries is no longer an issue that divides our political parties – they all agree. So campaigning investment is contributing to the generation of much greater Government spending on international aid now, than ever was the case in the past.

Without campaigning by organisations like CAFOD, Christian Aid and Oxfam it is unlikely that the Fairtrade Foundation would have achieved the impact it has on our buying habits; creating incremental increases in producer income in poor countries. In the UK in 2005, sales of products carrying the Fairtrade mark exceeded £195M (an increase from just under £17M in 1995). [4]*Fairtrade ensures that products sold with its mark deliver better prices, decent working conditions, local sustainability and fair terms of trade for both farmers and workers in the developing world. By requiring companies to pay above market prices, Fairtrade addresses the injustices of conventional trade, which traditionally discriminates against the poorest, weakest producers. It enables them to improve their lot and have more control over their lives.*

---

[4] *Italic paragraph* from www.fairtrade.org.uk

Similarly, campaigning by NGOs around the world has had an impact on the creation of the Millennium Development Goals by the United Nations (MDGs)[5] in 2000. The eight Goals - which range from *'halving extreme poverty'* to *'halting the spread of HIV/AIDS'* and *'providing universal primary education',* all *to be achieved by the target date of 2015* – form a blueprint agreed to by all the world's countries and all the world's leading development institutions. Halfway to the deadline, there has been clear progress towards implementing the Goals. But their overall success is still far from assured and it will depend in a large part on whether developed countries meet the promises they made to their aid commitments. However, there has undoubtedly been considerably more progress than would have occurred without the Goals being set.

Viewed as an investment, expenditure on education and campaigning is money very well spent.

---

[5] *Italic paragraph* from www.un.org/millenniumgoals

2

Ethiopia – A Thumbnail Sketch

The Federal Democratic Republic of Ethiopia has a population of 75 million and covers an area similar in size to Scandinavia. It is also Africa's oldest independent country. Italy attempted to invade in the 1890s but the attack was beaten off at the battle of Adua. This town, the location and focal point of my first visit, had played a significant part of the country's history. The Italians returned during the Second World War but with British backing the Ethiopians evicted them in 1941. Apart from these two minor incursions, Ethiopia remains the only African state that has never been colonised.

In 1582 when the rest of the Christian world changed from the Julian to Gregorian calendar, Ethiopia did not and has not since. So Ethiopia remains 7 years and 8 months behind the rest of the world and will celebrate its millennium in September 2007. Most international businesses and organisations that are based in the country operate under the western calendar to avoid confusion.

The majority of Ethiopians are either Christian or Muslim; the relative percentages of each vary from region to region, but overall around 25% or more of the population is thought to be Muslim and this proportion is growing. The majority of Christians belong to the Ethiopian Orthodox Church and the overall percentage of Catholics is low (at about 1%), although it is higher in the Tigray Region and parts of the south.

The long serving Emperor Haile Selassie was toppled in 1974 by a popular revolution which was then itself overtaken by the self proclaimed Marxist junta known as the Derg and led by Mengitsu Haile Mariam. Opponents of the Derg were killed and their property confiscated allowing defence spending to be escalated. The junta was eventually overthrown in 1991, since when the head of state has been Meles Zenawi, who was born near Adua. Meles was the architect of a new constitution that came into effect in 1994 after which he became prime minister, winning a second term in office in multi-party elections in 2000. He won again in 2005, despite a large swing to the opposition that was particularly noticeable in the cities and there were accusations of foul play. In the considerable unrest that followed, scores of people were killed and hundreds arrested. Since then the Government has consolidated its position; de-regulation has been permitted and press freedom has flourished while increasingly, attention has focused on improving the lives of both the rural and urban poor.

A growing mobile phone network is one example of major investment in infrastructure, but perhaps even more significant are the steps being made towards the development of a modern education system. This has contributed to an economy that can boast a recent growth record approaching 10% per annum. However two thirds of the population remains illiterate and 85% of the economy is built on agriculture which is very susceptible to climatic variations. Outside the cities the health service is poor; HIV/AIDS is prevalent with up to 10% of the population infected in some areas.

Ethiopia caught the world's attention in 1985 when the effects of a long term drought in the Northern Tigray and Amhara regions became the lead story in newspapers and television alike. This led to a massive response, including Bob Geldof's impatient appeals and the 'Live Aid' concert. Tigray has suffered droughts since, but none on the scale of that in the early eighties, the effects of which were reportedly made much worse by the communist Government of the day covering up the true seriousness of the problem.

Eritrea, which at that time was a province of Ethiopia, won its right to independence through a referendum after the overthrow of the Communists. Relations between the two Countries began well, but in the mid nineties they deteriorated; both sides becoming economically antagonistic and with seemingly petty border disputes flaring up. This sparring escalated into a full scale military conflict in 1999 in which tens of thousands were killed on both sides. Since early 2000 a tense ceasefire has held. This episode has resulted in major humanitarian and economic costs, together with forced conscription and mass expulsion of citizens on both sides. Something which to an outsider seems a pointless and petty dispute is now the source of great enmity between people who, after centuries of historic tension, had become allies in the fight for independence and recognition.

Additionally there is a tense and long standing relationship with neighbouring Somalia. Ethiopia had been visibly supporting the provisional Somali government as it resisted a threat from the Union of Islamic Courts (UIC) who effectively controlled much of Somalia including the capital Mogadishu until they were ejected by Government troops with significant support from the Ethiopian Army. It is planned that African Union forces will replace Ethiopian troops as a stabilizing presence in Somalia although continuing unrest has slowed down the Ethiopian withdrawal.

The situation is not helped by Eritrea's public backing for the UIC. The effect of all this is that the Ethiopian military capability which was downgraded in the 1990s, has now been rebuilt as the country reassesses the threat to its sovereignty. Ethiopia's military machine is much respected by other African states.

Behind all these issues I was to discover an unexpectedly beautiful country with friendly and mostly happy people, in spite of their historical turmoil and economic uncertainty.

3

November 2006 - Preparation

The preparation began a long time ago! In October 1966, whilst at University in Cardiff, a group of us organised a sponsored walk on behalf of OXFAM – these were early days for this type of fund-raising. We planned for a hundred or so walkers to join in and were completely overwhelmed when around 5,000 turned up. Thankfully the event passed off safely, raised several thousand pounds and generated significant local interest. It also gave me my very first experience of dealing with the media.

My interest in the third world continued as I graduated and embarked on a career in what was then called the Computer Industry. In 2002 I ended this career which had been as successful as I had hoped and began building a new life for myself by volunteering to help an assortment of Charities, one of which was CAFOD. Exploiting the communications skills I had developed in my first career I began to visit schools to give talks in classes and assemblies about the challenges faced by third world communities and the work of CAFOD in providing assistance.

In 2006 CAFOD sought volunteers to visit Ethiopia for two weeks with the prime purpose of generating media interest in the UK. I applied and was selected. For me this project offered two significant benefits: the opportunity to see at first hand the lives and challenges of people in the third world; and the chance to assess whether, through our donations to organisations such as CAFOD, we are making a difference.

And so, after a career, four daughters and eight grandchildren; and forty years on from my first interest in the third world I embarked on a journey that was completely outside my previous experience. Many people visit Ethiopia regularly – businessmen, aid workers, diplomats, journalists, health workers, and sportsmen; so my visit was really no big deal except that I was going with a completely fresh and open outlook. I wanted to be impressed with what I saw, but I also had the underlying semi-scepticism which meant that I would not accept anything I saw at face value.

* * * * *

Five of us went on the trip in November 2006. Paul Gill and I were the two volunteers; Paul having just completed his Masters degree at Sheffield University. We were joined by Claire Kirk and Seb Gordon from the CAFOD Media team. Claire was the organiser and Seb – fresh from completing the New York Marathon for CAFOD - was the cameraman. Seb was in the team because Yorkshire Television had agreed to feature Paul's experiences. The fifth participant was Catherine Leeson from CAFOD's Community Fundraising team. Catherine and Paul were both planning to take part in the Great Ethiopian Run, together with the local CAFOD staff from Addis Ababa. This 10km run is a major event in Ethiopia and their participation was seen as another catalyst that would generate media coverage.

Preparation consisted of the inevitable research into Ethiopia; in particular the parts of the country we were going to visit, the work being undertaken by CAFOD and particularly the partners through whom the work was being delivered. We also had to prepare ourselves both to ensure our safety in the political and physical environment of the country and to assure ourselves we had taken all the medical precautions to equip us for a different climate and way of life.

We started to blog[6]! This was a new idea for a trip of this type, but was to prove very worthwhile. The blog was <u>our</u> work, but CAFOD put a link to it from their home page, once they had satisfied themselves we were not going to say anything too contentious. They were keen to ensure that CAFOD did not become associated with anything we

---

[6] My blog can be read at http://cafodethiopia.blogspot.com/

published on the blog that might cause them embarrassment with partners or governments

To my surprise (the first of many surprises!) we were encouraged to contact local media (press and radio) to generate interest in the trip. I was very sceptical about the chance of success in this venture, wondering why anyone would want to know about some retired guy jetting off to Africa for two weeks. However I did what had been suggested and approached the list of media contacts that I'd prepared jointly with Claire. I was shocked by the response.

Several newspapers published articles about my proposed trip and every radio station I contacted wanted to interview me so two live studio sessions, one live telephone interview and three recorded conversations were booked. For a fledgling interviewee, the whole experience is a daunting one. Sitting behind a microphone for the first time not knowing what you are going to be asked, yet with a clear idea of what you want to say whatever the question was somewhat scary. Although I was very nervous at first, my confidence increased and by the third interview I actually began to enjoy them.

We left on the overnight Ethiopian Airways flight to Addis Ababa on 15th November 2006.

4

Addis Ababa

As day dawned we could see the Nile below us, a scene which was soon replaced by inspiring mountainous scenery. The land was greener than we had expected, especially as we flew closer to the capital city. Landing just after 7am there was a noticeable chill in the air as we disembarked. Addis Ababa is 2700 metres above sea level and we were all prepared for the altitude to have some sort of effect. I noticed nothing, although Catherine said she felt an immediate impact on her pulse and breathing. The real effect of the altitude was to hit us later.

At breakfast one morning in the Ghion hotel I realised that I had not brought my malaria tablets with me. So I bounded up the two flights of stairs to my room to retrieve them, an exercise from which I needed several minutes to recover. A sudden spurt of activity is one of the factors that can trigger the effects of altitude to become very apparent. Another annoying effect of altitude was the struggle to find sleep at night – I would wake up for some reason, expecting to drop off again right away - but then find myself still awake three hours later!

On our arrival we were taken to the Ghion by Jannie Oosthuizen. He and his wife Bev Jones share the position of Country Representative of the joint CAFOD/Trocaire office in the country. I should explain that Trocaire is the Irish equivalent of CAFOD. We soon learnt what a great deal was gained by all from Jannie and Bev's working arrangement. Between them they worked considerably more than the equivalent of one full time person. However, the arrangement suited them too as it allowed one of them to be available for the school runs of their two children Daniel and Ioan. In the coming two weeks I was to develop a close rapport with this family, particularly with Bev and Ioan who were to be with me for some of my time in Tigray. These were the first real aid workers I had met. They were committed, conscientious, people-focused and determined; in my old business world they would have been in the upper echelons of management.

Addis was busy, dusty and run down, yet it was relatively quiet compared with other cities of a similar size. It was swarming with people, many of whom seemed to swarm with little purpose; and the roads carried lots of blue minibuses, most of which appeared to be running on a wing and a prayer. There were some wide newly built roads and one or two very modern looking buildings. A Saudi Prince with an Ethiopian mother had invested heavily in the city and was the motivator for much of the modern architecture, including the Sheraton Hotel and a new but as yet unoccupied office block that dominated the city landscape next to the Ghion.

On arrival at the Ghion my first priority was to find some drinking water. We had been indoctrinated with the need to ensure we did not even start to become dehydrated and that we should not trust any source of water other than a sealed bottle. A 2 litre bottle was my first Ethiopian purchase from the Hotel bar and at 12 birr or 75 pence it was a relatively expensive one.

The Ghion was an old Government hotel, fairly basic but clean. It had individual bathrooms, although the availability of hot water was a lottery that I rarely won. I would have been disappointed if we had been staying anywhere more upmarket and expensive; I feel it's important that an aid Charity should ensure its staff and volunteers stay in adequate comfort but not in luxury. Throughout both my trips CAFOD judged this exactly right.

On the afternoon of our arrival and after a sleepless rest, Jannie took us to meet Daniel Hailu who is the programme coordinator for EIFFDA (Ethiopian Interfaith Forum on Development, Dialogue and Action), an organisation which aims to adopt common approaches to peace and reconciliation, food security and HIV/AIDS.

An impressive and gentle man, Daniel spoke with passion about his work. He gave the impression that inter-faith tolerance was generally good, but that there was very little actual co-operation. Daniel was going to accompany Paul, Claire and Seb on their visit to the flood affected region around Dire Dawa.

That first evening we had a quite palatable traditional Ethiopian meal in the hotel. The spicy food should have been eaten by picking up portions with a piece of injeera bread in the right hand. Unfortunately Seb, being left-handed, found himself automatically using the 'wrong' hand to pick up his food until the waitress told him rather abruptly to behave himself. We were all wary of eating too much unusual food, especially so early in the trip and following this meal my stomach felt quite strange. It never quite recovered and was to continue to feel odd throughout the whole trip, although miraculously I never developed any real gastric problems.

The next day started with a visit to the CAFOD/Trocaire office to meet with Jannie and the rest of the staff. Our pre-briefing on security and health topics was reinforced. Although much of the information was common sense it did no harm to remind us of the risks we might face and of the steps we should take to minimise them. After this we went to a local bistro for lunch, again being very careful what we ate and drank. We then hired a minibus for a drive around the city.

We drove up into the hills to an old church 1000 metres above the city where the views would have been spectacular were it not for the polluted haze sitting over the connurbation. As a first time visitor to Ethiopia, this drive left me with some of my strongest and most evocative memories of the country.

There were crowds of people including many children in very smart uniforms, some of whom broke from their main party to surround our minibus in an effort to persuade us to part with money. We saw a stream of people walking home up the hill away from the last bus stop beyond which the buses simply couldn't drive. Women almost jogged down the hill carrying enormous loads of eucalyptus branches that they had gathered to sell in the City.

That night we went to the Lalibella restaurant near the Ghion and ate conventionally. We were all keen and excited to get going with our real tour placements.

The next day I was due to leave for Adua in Tigray before dawn and Paul, Claire and Seb were off to Dire Dawa. Catherine was preparing to leave later for Mekelle in Tigray en route to her placement in Alitena, a town very close to the Eritrean border

    We were about to see the real Ethiopia.

5

Relief Society of Tigray

The real Ethiopia I was about to enter can be summarised by a few basic facts on Tigray. There are over 4 million people living in the province, 80% of whom live in rural areas where the majority are subsistence farmers producing on average less than half their annual minimum food requirements. Nearly 90% earn less than $2 per day and their average life expectancy is 43 years.

I had never been anywhere like this before and felt a strange mixture of apprehension, trepidation and excitement.

I said farewell to the others in the Addis Ababa internal flight departure lounge and was alone until I was met at Axum airport by Merid Alemayehu. Merid is the coordinator in Adua for the Relief Society of Tigray (REST), the CAFOD partner managing the project I was going to visit.

Axum was the last of four stops on the journey in a twin-engined propeller driven Fokker aircraft. At the first stop in Bahir Dar on the banks of Lake Tana, the source of the Nile, the plane broke down. The pilot started his engines, revved up and then cut them. We had all waited there for about half an hour when a luggage carrier started to offload our bags. Then about half the passengers stood up and left the 'plane while the rest of us remained seated. It seemed sensible that we should get off along with our luggage to lessen the chances of losing it, but to confirm this I asked one of the stewardesses whether we should leave. Her puzzling reply was, "That's your decision!" I think what she really meant was "This 'plane isn't going anywhere – you can either get off and stand in the sun or wait here in the relative cool while we sort out another 'plane". Not wanting to miss the backup aircraft, I got off.

Eventually there was another plane ready on the tarmac and after more delays we boarded it, finally arriving in Axum two and a half hours late. I was impressed by my own calmness, although I was a little worried by keeping Merid waiting for me as there was no way I could contact him. One lesson I learnt that day is that these things happen all the time in Ethiopia. Merid was there waiting for me and he welcomed me with a greeting that would have been just the same had I been on time.

REST owns a minibus which is used to visit the projects. Staff with expertise in different aspects of project work travel to and from the various locations which are spread over many square miles. The minibus was waiting for us at the airport ready to drive us into Axum itself. On the way I was surprised to pass an oil tanker emblazoned with the word TESCO on its side, but no, it was not the same TESCO. While we were driving Merid talked me through our schedule for the four days I was to be with him.

Merid is 38 years old and is married with two boys of 7 and 4. His family live in Mekelle, the capital of Tigray which has a population about the size of Reading; it is a good day's drive from his office in Adua. He only sees his family about every 4 weeks when he is able to combine a trip home with a visit to REST HQ which is also in Mekelle. Because of his solitary life he works most weekends so our first proper meeting would be the following morning, on Sunday. However, in the afternoon he was to be a guest at the wedding of one of his team and therefore we would not be able to meet. I understood entirely and said I would spend the afternoon at the Don Bosco compound in Adua where I had been billeted for this part of the trip.

I then had another surprise as he asked if I would like to go with him to the wedding. I thought perhaps he was embarrassed by having to leave me in order to attend the event and so had invited me out of a sense of duty. For that reason I tried not to appear too keen to go. On the inside I couldn't believe that I might have a unique opportunity to sample such an important piece of the country's culture. Finally Merid made it very clear that he would like me to go and it was perfectly alright with the happy couple.

The plan for the Saturday afternoon was that after we had stopped so I could buy another two litres of bottled water, this time for a more modest 4 birr, Merid would show me the historic sites of Axum.

I was really taken with the Stelae field of monolithic structures that were built around 2000 years ago. There are many excellent accounts of the sites of Axum and its associated museum so I will not try to emulate them here. They are fascinating enough to attract more tourists to the area and are a worthy addition to the churches of Lalibella which is the last stop before Axum on the plane journey from Addis Ababa.

My entry fee to the Axum historic sites was the princely sum of 50 birr (just over £4). As a local, Merid only paid 5 birr. This concept of Firenji (foreigner) pricing is prevalent in many areas and even includes internal air fares. This seems to me to be absolutely sensible and fair. For me, £4 was more than reasonable; although anything more than 5 birr for local people would mean that most would be unable to afford visits to their own heritage sites.

Those moments spent standing in the middle of the Stelae field linger in my memory as one of the pivotal points of the trip. It was not just because of the history on view, but because for the first of many times the vivid contrast between Ethiopia and the United Kingdom hit me hard.

The reality of Tigray was quite different from all the pre-conceptions that I had formed from photo's, television footage or talks from people who had been before. Unmade roads, swarming people, camels, goats and cattle all seemed oblivious to our presence. There was also some of the most stunning scenery I had ever seen. Yet the most striking thing was not the poverty or the dust, the begging or the beauty for I had expected all of these.

The thing that almost overwhelmed me was the silence. The tinnitus of industrialised background noise had been cured, with the effect of amplifying all the natural sounds. We could hear only the sounds of people chatting, children playing and animals – for miles around. I was at last in a different world.

After leaving the sites we drove 20 very bumpy kilometres to Adua. I braced myself on one occasion as the bus seemed to be leaving the road, only to realise that the driver was avoiding a large pot hole with which he was clearly very familiar. The scenery was spectacular and everyone waved. There seemed to be an unwritten rule that when passing the infrequent oncoming vehicles (usually mini-buses or Land Cruisers) the closing speed should be as great as possible and the passing gap as narrow as possible. Now I understood why I had to carry an accident emergency kit and a card which indicated my blood group. However the REST driver was highly competent and wouldn't budge until I was properly belted up. He even slowed down when I drank from my water bottle so that I didn't spill any.

I was dropped off at the Don Bosco Compound at about 5 in the afternoon and shown to my room by Brother Fabius. The room was simple but it had a toilet, a shower and a lovely view over the compound to the mountain beyond. As an indication of the wonderful friendliness of these people, as soon as they realised I'd had no food all day the Brothers rustled up some magnificent chips!

Don Bosco[7] was the founder of the Salesian Order which is committed to helping deprived young people from around the world. The Adua compound was dominated both by the Church which was built in the last ten years and the Technical College where young people are trained in construction, machine technology, computers and electrical engineering. The principal of the College who was also the senior 'Brother' was Father Tino. The compound also contained a junior school run by a local order of nuns.

The whole complex was opened up in the evening so that youngsters could attend to do their homework. It was quite impressive to see a steady stream of young people arriving and getting straight down to work. Overall I found the commitment and determination of the Don Bosco team very impressive. Their entire focus was to make a difference to the young people of the area. I was concerned to see the magnificent Church which was ten times larger and ten times grander than could be justified by the size of the Catholic population. However, it had been funded by wealthy Italians and not by the Salesians but I still couldn't help thinking the money should have been spent more wisely on facilities for the local people. There is something incongruous about a Church

---

[7] For more see www.salesians.org.uk/

deliberately designed to look good being built in an area of poverty and where most Churches are for the Orthodox congregations.

Father Tino was a larger-than-life Italian Priest, full of energy, wisdom and not a little mischief. He had been in Adua for some years and was looking forward to retirement, although I think in his case that would mean a change of scenery rather than a rest. He explained that education was beginning to develop in the villages, where most of the population is to be found, but some parents were still reluctant to release their children from farming duties. I was to discover later that it is not unusual for grandparents to replace children on the farm to allow them to go to school.

There is an electricity supply in Axum and Adua that comes complete with the inevitable cuts; it was when one of these occurred that I realised I should have packed a torch. Father Tino explained how the power supply had been built by an Indian Company and that for the villages the real hope for power was in a new type of solar panel. Dinner at Don Bosco's was frugal but wholesome; a mix of Ethiopian and Italian fayre washed down with Ethiopian beer for which I was already beginning to get a taste.

* * * * *

REST[8] developed from the humanitarian wing of the Tigray People's Liberation Front (TPLF), the political party which now forms the core of the national Government and is now a regional development organisation with strong and lasting links to the party. REST has often been viewed as more powerful than local government, however it is increasingly engaging with and even learning from other organisations including the Catholic Church. CAFOD has had a long involvement with REST beginning in the years of the civil war and the Eritrean war of independence when they channeled significant amounts of UK funding for REST's major humanitarian contribution.

The organisation's overall goal is '*to bring about a sustainable improvement in food and secure livelihoods within their operational areas*'. It sees the key components of the work needed to achieve this goal as the improvement of water supply and security, health, education and the

---

[8] For more see http://www.rest-maret.org/

empowerment of women. These activities should strengthen household livelihoods and contribute to REST's promotion of sustainable natural resource management.

I was to learn much more about REST during my two visits. I would meet many of their staff, both at Headquarters and out in the field. Overall they have achieved an enormous amount in recent years and can rightly be proud of the progress they have made towards their goal.

The following morning, Merid collected me in the minibus to take me to the REST office in the centre of Adua. He was resplendent in a smart suit ready for the wedding and looked a little out of place in my first glimpse of the dusty town. I resolved to find some time to walk around it on my own but regrettably time constraints meant that this would never happen. That morning the town was alive with people going to (mainly Orthodox) Church; although in various corners young boys were occupied with the international language of football, which was alive and well in Adua, despite a very small population of television sets.

Merid

The office was much as I would have expected. It was old, run-down and surrounded by rough ground. The sparse furniture wouldn't have made it to a car boot sale back at home. The office technology comprised one or two very old computers and a single telephone. The walls were covered with flip charts full of information about local projects; they were complete with actions, target dates for completion and progress notes. We went from chart to chart as Merid explained the watershed projects to me. This was a thoroughly professional briefing, even more noteworthy considering that it was not conducted in his native tongue. Merid gave every indication of being a man with total belief in his work and absolute commitment to it. He also enjoyed talking about it. From that moment I had little doubt that funding REST was a good decision and my inherent scepticsm was largely eliminated.

The 'Adua Sustainable Community-Managed Development Project' – the formal title of the watershed projects – has as its general objective the rehabilitation of the natural resource base to improve food security in the four targeted watersheds on a sustainable basis. This general objective can be broken down into specific items as follows:

1. Improve water conservation and irrigation to increase both agricultural productivity and diversification while improving access to safe drinking water.
2. Reduce soil erosion.
3. Increase and diversify off-farm income sources, particularly for households headed by women.
4. Improve family health and the nutritional status of the targeted community.
5. Contribute to creating greater access to education, particularly in remote areas.
6. Create awareness of the issues around the spread and prevention of HIV and AIDS
7. Promote women's equality in participation and access to benefits.

The activities underway to achieve the above objectives were numerous. They included clean water schemes, water flow management, re-forestation work, horticultural development, livestock development, health education and community capacity building. All this work sits comfortably with REST's overall objectives.

The population of the Adua Woreda (District) was about 130,000 of which about 17,000 lived in the area covered by the project. I could see that for the 17,000 potential beneficiaries the results of the project would be life-saving and life-changing. It also occurred to me that for them to play their part in making the project successful, they would have to change, as an act of faith, the way they live and work and that in so doing they would improve the quality of their lives still more.

The project ran for three years from April 2004 and cost about 10million birr. The funding came from a consortium of The European Union, CAFOD, Trocaire and Christian Aid, with the management on behalf of the Consortium being performed by the Ethiopian joint CAFOD/Trocaire Office. Later that evening I did a simple sum. I calculated that the amount of 10 million birr (£625,000) to transform the lives of 17000 people over a 3 year period cost about £1 per person per month. For this trifling sum they would get clean water, irrigation, better health and education and a chance to enhance their routine income. What a fantastic deal that is!

Following Merid's briefing I was left eager to get out and see the watersheds for myself – but we had a wedding to go to. As my concession to formality and in the absence of a jacket, I put on a tie for the journey to Axum.

* * * * *

Weddings in Tigray are long-drawn-out affairs, lasting over several days. On the first day there is the Orthodox Church service; followed on the next day by the formal ceremony which is the part I was able to attend. The ceremony begins around lunchtime with everyone except the bride assembling over a period of a couple of hours at the house of the groom's parents. There is eating, drinking, singing, some dancing and a lot of chatting and children running riot. Then the party progresses to the home of the bride's parents and is greeted with a lot of noise and more dancing. Inside there is more food and drink for the adults. The groom then disappears into the depths of the house and returns with his bride for the formal ceremony. The central party then sits down to eat while everyone else continues to mingle, dance and chat well into the evening until the guests begin to drift away. After the day of the ceremony the bride and groom stay with the bride's parents for three days, then everyone assembles again at the groom's parents' house for another party!

At about midday we drove down a narrow track to the groom's parent's house. Outside was a special area covered with a large tarpaulin to keep the sun at bay; in the shade of the makeshift roof were benches on which people sat in shifts. Food and the local brew were served to those seated, whilst a couple of musicians wandered among the benches. Every now and then people playing instruments that looked like metal pipes led in some of the more important guests who were welcomed with the traditional greeting sound called ululisation, which is made somehow from the back of the throat. There was a lot of kissing and cuddling, presumably between the two sets of wider families and the whole process continued until about 3.30.

Merid was a superb host, although at first I didn't let him out of my sight. He was my lifeline as I was the only firenji at the wedding. Throughout the event he explained to me with great patience about everything that was happening and seemed to turn a blind eye to my unsuccessful attempts to simulate eating and drinking. I'm afraid the appearance of all the refreshments left me feeling more than a little queasy. I could just about give the appearance of eating some food by taking chunks of injeera but I was more easily able to avoid the drink by putting it on the floor under the bench. Looking back on the day, I recall seeing the 'Happy Wedding' signs in English, the respect shown to the elders as they arrived, the smiling faces of the children, the repetitive music that still sings in my head and the apparently chaotic organisation which was almost certainly more disciplined than it appeared. To me, the whole experience was enthralling.

Twice during this period Merid took me out for a break. We went for coffee at the main hotel, which was very civilised. As the prices were set for firenji I offered to pay but was firmly rebuffed. Later we walked along the main street where there was no traffic, just camels, donkeys and goats. Small untidy shops selling a variety of produce lined the street; surprisingly many of them were selling Premiership football scarves – the most prolific of which was that of Arsenal FC. There are only a few televisions in the town, but when football is on all the kids migrate towards them. It left me thinking how great an opportunity there was to exploit this enthusiasm for the game by engaging British fans to help their counterparts in the third world and for the teams themselves to thrill their remote fans by visiting.

The journey from the groom's house to the bride's could have been done in about five minutes but it must have taken over half an hour. The few vehicles in the party drove round the town several times with horns honking and followed by the rest of the party on foot. At the bride's parents' house we were greeted by her 'intimate friends', whom we would call bridesmaids, all stunning in red dresses. Both parties danced together for several minutes and it was at this point I was pleased that Merid let his hair down and joined in. By then I had met other members of the REST staff, and although most appeared not to speak English, at least I could recognise a few more friendly faces.

We then went inside again, or rather under another tarpaulin; and were ushered to one of the few benches which I assumed were reserved for close family and friends. I was introduced to several elders who seemed very keen to make me feel welcome. Merid explained that guests in Tigray were always treated as if they were angels from heaven. Once again refreshments appeared for the guests on the benches and once again I prepared for the pretence of eating. It must have been obvious I was finding the food a struggle, so on the assumption that it was too spicy someone with the best of intentions arranged for me to have my own version without the spices. Unfortunately my guardian angel had misunderstood the problem; I like spicy food - my difficulty was with the things that had been spiced. The replacement dish, for instance was later identified as sheep's intestines. I had just decided that I'd have to eat it, when the wise elders saw my predicament, gave the dish to some children and produced a bottle of Fanta for me.

After this came the ceremony, which I recorded on my camcorder, but as I feared it was too dark for a good result and the pictures that had looked acceptable on the miniscreen turned out to be very poor when transferred to the computer. I managed one very good still of the happy couple in which the shy bride gave a rare smile so I later mailed some copies out to Merid. I was never made to feel an outsider by constant stares although the children found my camcorder a strange and compelling object. Seeing themselves on the miniscreen caused loud and excited whoops and giggles among the youngsters.

At about 6-30 p.m. Merid said that I should return to Adua with the minibus and the other REST staff. As the groom was one of his staff Merid would stay until the end of festivities at about 11 p.m. During the journey the staff replayed my video of the event giving shrieks of delight at seeing themselves on the screen. It was dusk as we drove along the now familiar road from Axum to Adua, with the dying light rendering the scenery even more stunning than before.

Back at Don Bosco's I was grateful to be in time for dinner. Throughout the meal I must have bored the Brothers with my stories of the unique local cultural event I had been privileged to be part of. To cap a wonderful day I discovered that they had a really good internet connection which meant I would be able to blog throughout my stay.

6

Adua - The Watersheds

Monday dawned with the promise of a perfect day; cloudless skies with a little haze over the mountain. Complete with my back pack filled with sun cream, insect repellent, emergency kit, toilet roll, water and medicines to counter dietary problems, somehow I was ready early. I felt like a lunar explorer about to go on a moon walk with his life support system on his back.

We went initially to the local REST office where I met up with many of the team who had been to the wedding; while Merid did some organising for the day. We then left together with one of the lady staff members, an agricultural expert from Mekelle. The drive to the St Michael Watershed took about half an hour including a stop to pick up Assefa Weldemarian who was the Chairman of the Watershed Committee. The work of the project is not just overseen by the funders but by the local community who benefit from it. The Committee is the vehicle for ensuring the community's full involvement.

We got out of the minibus at a sign that described the project and its funders. Assefa strode off over the rough land with Merid, his team members and me in hot pursuit. I decided that our lady colleague must not have known she was going to spend the day walking through farmland and countryside as she was wearing heeled shoes that were far from ideal. To her credit she never flagged or complained. I was grateful to be reasonably fit as the pace was quite quick over the very rough ground and it was also getting hot. I was wearing a thin long sleeved shirt but the others all had on some sort of jacket as well; for them this was the coolest time of the year. After about a mile and a half we stopped at the edge of a gully. It was dry but every few metres inside the gully were block dams.

Assefa on a Block Dam

Tigray has an average rainfall of 600 mm per year most of which falls between June and August, usually in a small number of very heavy outbursts. This kind of rainfall doesn't soak into the ground; it creates torrents that rush away very quickly eroding a lot of the soil as they go. The natural springs do not get properly replenished and the streams can run dry within a few weeks. Prior to the project, access to water was from these unreliable streams which were also used by animals. In some years, most notably 1985 when little or no rain fell, the area has been stricken by drought and dependent upon emergency aid relief.

Merid was at High School in 1985 and remembers very well what happened. Everyone tried to get to the towns where they expected to find food and water but many died in the attempt. He told me about a baby girl who was saved just minutes from death and is now a fully qualified engineer. This was the same girl that Bob Geldof introduced to the Live 8 Concert twenty years later.

The prime objective of the St Michael Watershed project is to protect the supply of water. The gully I was looking into had been dug out by the villagers to create a channel to direct the water to the point that it could best feed a natural spring. The block dams were made by filling gabion frames with local stone, creating a solid wall across the gulley. Positioned expertly, these block dams slowed down the flow of water considerably, ensuring more was channeled into the spring and underwater aquifers and that the soil erosion was reduced. The effort expended to build this system must have been enormous; the local farmers and villagers having done it themselves after the previous harvest period in November and December. The fact that they were motivated to do it owes much to the ability of the experts in the project who explained to them the benefits it had the potential to produce.

We followed the gully down to the spring, past piles of rocks that had been collected ready to build more block dams to increase the depth of the gulley once the harvest was over. The spring was producing a generous supply of water. Through an underground pipe connected directly to the source, pure drinking water was being carried further downstream to a very large underground tank that fed three stand pipes. These outlets were the water source for the 1750 villagers in the area and were no more than 30 minutes walk from any home. The spring also fed an open stream where women were washing clothes and a donkey was drinking whilst its owner filled containers from the taps. No wonder there was a smile on the face of the owner's son who was minding the donkey. There was plenty of water and it was clearly drinkable. I was left musing that stand pipes for these villagers indicated phenomenal progress – stand pipes for us in Britain would be seen as a disaster.

Irrigation channels came both from the stream and from the water tank overflow. The channels were directed towards fertile areas where a wide range of crops were growing. The staple crops here are 'sorghum' and 'teff' from which the injeera bread is made. However these staple crops were supplemented by sesame oil seed that was grown for export, tomatoes, peppers, chillies, mangoes, onions, lettuce and many others. This diversity gave the farmers much greater income potential than they could achieve by just growing the staple crops. We were almost back to the road when we were shown a pump that was extracting water from a 53 metres deep well, providing yet another pure source.

Across the road was a school for 7 to 9 year-olds which had been built by the community 2 years previously using local stone they had collected. The Government had funded all the other materials needed in the construction and the project had included a rainwater capture system with two large storage tanks which provided water for drinking and washing. 8 teachers worked with about 340 children in morning and afternoon shifts in only three classrooms. The children were all busy as we entered each class, but when they saw me they immediately shouted 'welcome' in unison. The classroom walls were covered with pictures, words and numbers in English as well as the local Tigrayan language. There were desks for younger children, but the 9 year-olds were sitting on the floor. I was left in no doubt that education was a Government priority; here was a remote part of the country and the children were walking to a new school with enthusiasm despite the distances involved. There was a plan to extend the school, providing classes for 10 year-olds and ending the very long walk to Adua that currently faces many of the pupils each day.

Just along from the school were two elders tending to several goats; visible evidence of grandparents who had returned to work to release children from farm work so that they could access education.

We then moved back into farmland to meet a family that was headed by Priest Seuyam. A 78 year old farmer and Orthodox Priest, he had lived on the same piece of land all his life. It would have been marvelous to talk to him about his life and the changes he had observed over the years but this was one of many occasions when there wasn't the time to dig deeper into the lives of Tigrayan people. Priest Seuyam looked younger than his 78 years; a real example of how working can keep you young. He showed us some sugar beet, which his wife (whose age I didn't ask) had brought back from friends some distance away. Her planting had been successful and the beet was growing well as yet another crop diversification opportunity. The Priest's wife appeared with food for us; injeera and a chick pea dip were really quite appetizing!

Throughout the day I had been pausing frequently to drink from my water bottle but I realised that Merid and the others were not only still wearing coats despite the heat but had drunk nothing at all.

We walked down the valley a little and met the Priest's daughter, Ngisti and her 9 year-old son, Gidey. At 42, Ngisti was a single mum and although I didn't ask what had happened to Gidey's father, the most likely answer was that he had died, like so many of his generation, in the conflict with Eritrea. The project here focused more effort on households that were headed by women and it had provided Ngisti with a cow that had high milk yield potential. These cows provided by the project came from the west of Tigray and on average they produced eight litres of milk a day, double that of the local breeds. Ngitsi's cow was financed on credit which would have to be repaid after five years; the milk yield should mean that this is entirely possible. She had also been provided with a modern beehive. As it was populated by a very aggressive swarm it was not wise to get too close; the compensation was in the delicious honey she gave me to taste. Ngisti also grew a range of vegetables giving her a very broad income base. The situation of Ngisti and Gidey summed up the whole benefit of the project. They had a life. It was a hard life but they had clean water, a variety of income sources and Gidey could go to school.

With Ngisti and Gidey

Back in the office Merid and I spoke about marketing. The project's focus to date had rightly been on establishing the sustainable production of a variety of farm produce; however it was now time to work out how to distribute and sell the produce beyond the village boundaries. There was an identified demand for vegetables, dairy products and the quality honey produced by people like Ngisti in their subsidised hives. The challenge was to work out how to balance the relatively short shelf life of these products with the opportunity to sell them beyond the weekly Saturday market in Adua. Merid had attended some basic marketing training at REST HQ and recognised that developing a marketing plan is the key to the future. More than that, marketing needs to be a fundamental part of any bid for additional funding for the project once the current budget is exhausted in 2007.

I was taken back to Don Bosco's by the REST driver, more than a little tired but completely exhilarated by everything I had seen. Merid was one of the more fortunate Ethiopians; he was very well educated and had a good grasp of English, although he became a little confused sometimes when my own questions were less than straightforward or direct. Merid seemed totally motivated by a desire to help those among his fellow citizens who were much less well off than he was.

* * * * *

On the next morning which was Tuesday, we drove to the much larger Tsigereda watershed to the east of Adua with at least one lesson already learnt; our lady colleague was wearing appropriate shoes. We began the day in a village where I was taken into a particularly ramshackle building to meet two quite lively men. Merid explained that the project had arranged for them to be trained in metalwork, primarily to build cattle pens which I was to see later. However they had used their new found skills in a completely different way by building a baking oven.

Despite the home made appliance not being wired to the same Health and Safety standards we would impose in Britain, they now bake 1700 large rolls every night. The delicious bread is eagerly bought by their fellow villagers for 25 cents or just over 1p per roll. They explained their plans to increase production by extending it into daylight hours and how they were saving their 400 birr profit each month so that they could find or build a proper bake house rather than renting the old building we were in. During the few minutes we were chatting the queue of people waiting to buy bread had grown to ten. Here was a shining example of how a little help had unleashed an inherent spirit of enterprise and self-sufficiency. Like people the world over, these two wanted to make something of their lives, to better themselves and their families; all they needed was some expertise and encouragement.

Further along the track we went into another building where two more men were churning milk to produce butter and cream. Local milk production generated largely from the high yield cows supplied on credit now exceeded demand, so the excess was turned into dairy products. Having a longer shelf life than milk, these could be taken to the Saturday market in town. In the same building the wife of one of the men brewed tea for sale to the villagers. She had two prices – 30 cents for tea and an additional 70 cents to take it with milk. She also brewed a local milky drink that was a little sweet but also spicy hot. She gave Merid and me a mug each and I sipped it cautiously, but it was delicious. I suggested to Merid that it would be hard to process the drink for export , but maybe the recipe should be patented and sold to European coffee shops.

Walking even further we passed a poster that was aimed at increasing the awareness of the risk of HIV/AIDS. It showed examples of the practices which increased the risk as well as the steps that could be taken to reduce them. The poster was quite explicit and therefore a little shocking, reminding me of some of the anti smoking campaigns at home. Later, when thinking about this more deeply, I realized that of all the people I had met, I had seen none of them smoking.

I was to see more posters as hard hitting the first. One was a parody of the three wise monkeys which was aimed at encouraging people to be open about AIDS and not to pretend it didn't exist. Another was aimed at changing the conventional thinking about the role of women. Its premise was that fetching water, milking cows and doing the washing was not necessarily all that women could do and indeed there was no reason why they should not have help with those chores as well. Merid explained that the project had run gender awareness courses which had been attended by both men and women. He said that the men were quite receptive to the new way of thinking, but I suspect that the real change will only happen when the current younger generation who have the training but not the same traditional mind set, start families of their own. I decided that when I finally get home I ought to learn how to operate the automatic washing machine.

The farmers' training centre that was built by the project, is where the villagers received training in water conservation techniques, the growing of new crops and other subjects already mentioned. Next to it was the veterinary station, an essential service but as yet with only a part time vet. Adjoining it was a cattle pen with a bottleneck exit through which the cattle were driven to receive their injections.

We walked some way from the track to a small house, beside which was a small brick construction housing a pit latrine. The latrine was a two cubic metre hole in the ground covered by a solid concrete slab, in the middle of which was a hole that could be capped with a concrete insert. Through the brickwork a pipe rose up from the hole to allow the gases to escape. The villagers had built the small building; the slab and pipe work were supplied by the project. There were many households with these new toilet facilities, but many more had yet to be provided. To us in the West they are primitive, but for these people they are a giant step forward from having to use open ground with all the inherent risks of disease.

It was time to be driven again, this time off the track and into open country. We met the Chairman of the Tsigereda Watershed Committee and walked upstream for a couple of miles. Again the scenery was magnificent and the pure sounds of people and animals could be heard against the silence even though some must have been over a mile away. We were walking along another system of gullies and dams, although here, to reduce soil erosion, eucalyptus trees beside the gully had been felled and elephant grass had been planted along the banks. Elephant grass has a wonderful ability to spread, its roots creating a binding effect that helps prevent break-up of the gully walls when the rain becomes torrential. When elephant grass is cut down to be fed to the cattle this further enhances its ability to spread.

This was a larger water system than the one at St Michael's Watershed, and included a large check dam. This was a very solid concrete structure that could be manually opened and closed.

Towards the top of the gully the floor was covered in rocks. Merid explained that this was the remains of a block dam which hadn't been built in gabion frames. It had been washed away and would therefore need to be rebuilt before the next rainy season. When asked why gabion frames had not been used he explained that it had become too expensive and the project could no longer afford it. Later he showed me the current prices of gabion and I was surprised at just how much it cost. This was the first and only example I found where the project had failed but the cause was market forces outside its control and the block dam could be rebuilt. Until I saw how expensive the gabion was I had the wild and fleeting idea of doing some fundraising for it when I got home. About £20,000 of gabion was needed on site, and I felt this was too large a sum to be raised quickly; there were also many more pressing uses for that amount of money

I was then introduced to Tekle Haimanot, who was described by Merid as a 'model farmer'. He had an enormous diversity of crops ranging from a small herb garden through traditional sorghum and hay right up to an orchard of avocados and coffee. He had built a storage hut designed to prolong the life of his vegetables once they had been harvested and had dug his own little reservoir which was fed from the gulley. A foot pump was used to extract water from the reservoir to be channeled into his irrigation system. The pump had been provided by the project and was designed to be easily dismantled for cleaning and maintenance. Tekle was a larger than life character who gave me lots of information about everything that he did and at such a pace that I'm sure Merid managed to translate only a small portion of it.

We had come a long way since leaving our vehicle; it was hot and I had developed blisters from walking over the rough terrain. I prepared myself for another long walk back, but was delighted to see that the minibus had found a way to get to us. The drive back was even bumpier than normal, but much preferred to walking!

I was dropped back at Don Bosco's at about 4 pm. Father Tino was going to drive me to Axum at 5. The previous evening Bev Jones had arrived and was spending the day with another CAFOD partner near Axum. Bev was accompanied by her younger son Ioan who is 4 and her friend Jackie. Jackie was officially on holiday but doubled as a child minder for Ioan when Bev had business meetings. Her husband Jannie was in Addis, also at work, but able to take the older son to and from school. We met at a hotel overlooking the Axum stelae and then went for an Ethiopian meal to the other firenji hotel, where Merid had taken me for coffee during the wedding. Father Tino enjoyed baiting Ioan who was more intelligent and inquisitive than one would expect for his age. After the meal, Father Tino and I drove back to Adua which was to be my last journey along this bumpy but picturesque road.

That evening I sent what I expected to be my final blog until arrival back in Addis Ababa. As well as my normal daily diary I produced a short blog as requested by one of my local papers, but I sent it out to all my media contacts. The breakfast presenter at BBC Radio Northampton emailed me to say she had read it out on air.

It said:

CONTRASTS BETWEEN UK AND TIGRAY

8 a.m. in the UK: people are showering, watching TV, eating breakfast, driving to school and work and talking about Big Brother. Stand still outside and you hear a great hubbub of traffic on the road and in the air.

8 a.m. in Tigray: people are walking to collect their water, eating a small lump of bread, walking to school (if there is one near enough) and talking about how their crops are doing. Stand still outside and you hear - nothing - except chattering people and animal footsteps. The silence is deafening.

Life here is stark, but it is improving, although more can be done. I am going to learn a lot more about this whilst here. And yet you see a lot of smiling faces - on poor but very attractive people. Who's to say that we are actually better off in the UK.

* * * * *

The following morning I said farewell to the Don Bosco Brothers, but not before Father Tino had given me a whistle-stop tour of his technical college, pausing longest to see a little of the work done to help some of the disabled youngsters in the Community.

At the REST office around 9am on the Wednesday, Merid was organising the day while I had another look around the wall charts which meant so much more to me now I had been on walkabout. We then left with a younger lady member of the team and headed for the Woreda Administration (District Council) Office. This was larger than the REST office, but of a similar age and construction and it was where I was introduced to Ato Dejen Berhe.

Following my earlier briefing on the relative power and resources of REST compared with the local government offices, I was looking for signs of tension between Dejen and Merid. The whole conversation was about how the two organisations worked together to assess the needs of the community and how they could address them together in an agreed order of priority. The school I had visited was quoted by Dejen as an example of where the two organisations and the community had worked really well together. The only point of contention was that each would like the other to do more, but in reality they recognised the limitations both sides had to deal with.

99% of the Woreda budget came from central government, the remainder was the limited amount generated from local taxation. They had 900 employees, 56% of whom were teachers, a significant proportion that would continue to grow. Only 8% of Woreda was covered by the four watershed projects, but although some parts do not have the topography for similar projects there is plenty of scope to extend the methodology. Dejen felt that there was potential for up to 100 watersheds.

Watching their body language carefully, and allowing for the fact that some of Dejen's words were being translated, I concluded that the relationship between the two was healthy. It certainly felt better than some equivalent relationships between statutory and voluntary sectors that I have observed in Britain.

We then moved to the offices of the Department of Agriculture, the local outpost of a Central Government department. This was a shorter and more stilted conversation. The impression I had was that this department's involvement was only to see that agricultural training was as effective as possible. The relationship seemed a little tense, but was also less important for the health of the project than the previous one.

At both offices every door carried a poster with the public servants' Code of Conduct printed on it:

- INTEGRITY
- TRANSPARENCY
- ACCOUNTABILITY
- LOYALTY

- HONESTY
- CONFIDENTIALITY
- EXERCISING LEGITIMATE AUTHORITY
- SERVING THE PROFESSIONAL INTEREST
- IMPARTIALITY
- RESPONSIVENESS
- EXERCISING LEADERSHIP

These are fine words which, if put into practice, would ensure a public service devoid of corruption; effective, efficient and delivering great added value. I have no way of knowing to what extent these ideas are becoming embedded in the culture of the staff. Cynics might say that the fact they were printed in English as well as the local language meant they were really aimed at convincing the world that action was being taken to weed out corruption. I felt that whatever the motive for the wide display of the code, which I saw again in the University and once more in the Museum in Addis Ababa, it would certainly do more good than harm. I view it as a positive indication that the Government was genuinely trying to do the right thing.

A cellular 'phone service had been introduced into much of Tigray about a month before my visit and as we left the Government office I received a call. It was a line-testing call from BBC 3-Counties radio, following an email they had sent me the day before to set up a live interview on a programme hosted by Martyn Coote, who as far as I know is not related to me. The interview was scheduled for 9am UK time (noon in Tigray) and the line was perfect, so once we arrived back at the REST office I waited outside in readiness.

What followed was one of the most bizarre moments of the trip. I was patched into Martyn's previous item which was about charging for traffic congestion in Buckinghamshire. He then switched me in and by asking where I was he gave me the chance to talk about the very different sounds that surrounded me. The interview lasted several minutes during which I was able to describe what I had seen in the previous two days. I hope it came across in a way that showed just how much difference relatively small amounts of UK money can make to the lives of poor people in Africa, but I felt a million miles away from the world of the news item that had preceded the interview.

There were few local people with 'phones as I'm sure the cost would have been prohibitive for the majority. Merid was hoping to get one from a contact who was going to visit Addis, where the prices were likely to be at their lowest.

Bev, Ioan and Jackie arrived and after lunch at the only firenji hotel in Adua I said farewell to Merid, although we would be meeting again at REST HQ in Mekelle the following Friday.

The watersheds were the main part of the trip for me. I seemed to have crammed an enormous amount into four days and my understanding of the way the aid process worked and the benefits it could bring had taken a quantum leap.

The next part of the plan was for us to go via the Cathedral town of Adigrat to the village of Alitena close to the border with Eritrea, where Catherine had undertaken her assignment, before moving to the Tigrayan Capital of Mekelle, from where we would fly back to Addis Ababa.

7

Adigrat, Alitena and Mekelle

We left Adua at about 2pm in a Toyota Land cruiser driven by Solomon along a tortuously rough and winding road which was being widened from a single lane and otherwise improved in certain places by the Chinese Government. When finished it would still not be properly surfaced and would therefore not even qualify for ''B' Road status in Britain. We stopped briefly to see the old Temple at Yeha. The scenery here and along the whole route was even more stunning than that between Axum and Adua. In one direction the view from the temple was of a fertile land being harvested and in the other it was of rugged mountains in the shape of lions' heads. As we got closer to Adua the skies became very overcast, spoiling my opportunity of successfully photographing the landscape extravaganza. As we arrived at the Cathedral and Seminary in the middle of the town it began to rain.

We were billeted in cells in the seminary. These are small rooms with a bed and a wash basin and are more than adequate for one night; however it was important to remember how many doors to pass along the corridor before reaching the toilet, should it be needed in the torch less dark of the African night.

We had a short meeting with the Bishop of Adigrat, whom Bev clearly knew well. He was an impressive man, younger than me and with a broad perspective on the many challenges faced by the Tigrayan people. He came across as sensitive to the beliefs of all faiths, particularly his Orthodox and Muslim colleagues. He was genuinely interested in our trip and wanted to know abut my visit to Adua. He allowed Ioan to borrow his large collection of pens and to draw quietly on paper on the corner of his desk. Whatever one's faith it would have been be hard not to enjoy the company of this man and to respect his humanity.

The Bishop invited us to join him and his Seminary teaching staff for what turned out to be a very good dinner with plenty of beer and wine on the table. He introduced us all to his team and seemed to say an enormous amount about me although the only word I recognized apart from my name was 'BBC'.

After breakfast the next morning Jackie and I took a short personal tour around the very impressive Cathedral. Afterwards I went for a short walk which included a visit to the roof of the seminary. From here it was possible to look down over the town and watch a steady stream of children of every age, all in the same uniform, wending their way to school.

The journey to Alitena took about three hours through the same exciting landscape. On the way we stopped at a large dam that had been constructed by the German and Swiss Caritas organisations. As we got closer to the border we went through a military checkpoint, then a mile or so later Solomon stopped the car at a barrier across the road. With some glee he informed us that this was the Eritrean border, which we were not supposed to have gone near. We said "jolly good," and encouraged him to turn round and take the road to Alitena. I remembered reading on the FCO web site before leaving home, 'on no account go within 25 kilometres of the Eritrean border.' Well, Alitena was within that distance anyway, but we had gone to within a few feet!

Alitena is a very small town nestled between several mountains. There was not much farm land and it wasn't immediately obvious how anyone would be able to eke out a living. The setting was magnificent but that wouldn't buy food. We arrived at the small complex of the Daughters of Charity which had been connected to the electricity supply within the previous few weeks and, at the time we were there, also had a water supply.

We were given a great welcome by Sister Bisrat and offered drinks and injeera bread. As it was her lunch break, Catherine then appeared with Sister Ababa who ran the kindergarten. I felt a bit of an intruder into her assignment and was really privileged to have the opportunity to glimpse her trip as well as my own. I think when she saw us she felt a little sad as it indicated that the time to leave was approaching. We spent some time talking about our respective experiences in what seemed like the lifetime since we had been in Addis. Catherine then went back to the kindergarten, where she had spent much of her time in the previous few days.

The Daughters of Charity were set up in 1973 in response to a famine. They are now heavily involved in health and social work having shifted their emphasis in recent years away from relief and emergency response into development. As well as the kindergarten they run a health clinic which treats over 16,000 patients each year. With poor roads and no vehicular transport it can take up to 9 hours to reach the clinic yet mothers bring their babies to be weighed, monitored and immunised; at the same time they are given information on general health and hygiene. The sisters also encourage women to be enterprising. There are many women who have been left to bring up their children alone, primarily as a result of the war with Eritrea. The lives of many have been transformed by gardening here, growing vegetables for food for themselves and their children and also to sell in the local market.

We went into the kindergarten to see Catherine and the sisters at work with the children, who were wonderfully well behaved and very bright. One was able to complete a jigsaw of a map of Africa, even naming many of the countries as he put them in their right places. We disturbed the Montessori calm with our cameras, which as usual, entranced the children. Realising that our presence was a little disruptive and probably not entirely welcome we left Catherine and Sister Ababa to their work and were taken on a guided tour of the village by Sister Bisrat. We walked around, stopping at the Orthodox Church and the school for older children. It was really hard to appreciate just how much effort the children made to attend the School; this was the centre of a wide area of small sprawling villages, and some travelled over 20 miles each day on foot.

Our main stop was at the Health Clinic run by the Daughters of Charity. At the time we were there not much was going on as the morning clinic had finished and there were no in-patients. It was a little weird to see a small ward of four beds, in a third world country, all empty!

The Daughters of Charity were very concerned with the worsening problem of HIV/AIDS, and we spoke about this aspect of their work. They explained that AIDS testing is a two-stage process, because the disease can develop for around three months before it produces a positive test result. Despite this difficulty they were trying to persuade as many people as possible to take the test to establish their status. A lot of care was taken to ensure confidentiality; the counselor being chosen to ensure that he or she was not known to the villagers attending the clinic. Reduction of the stigma associated with the disease and offering advice to those affected and to their partners were both very important parts of the work.

The Catholic Church does not support the use of condoms as contraceptives, a policy that the Sisters supported by not distributing condoms to affected couples. This is a difficult topic for the Church whose position is very hard to comprehend for non-Catholics. However the Church's response to the disease is driven by a strong compassion for those infected and for those affected. The sisters will ensure that those living with HIV or AIDS are helped to consider all options open to them in deciding how to manage the rest of their lives.

After the tour we returned to the Sisters' compound where a large number of women had assembled for a regular meeting facilitated by the sisters. Most of the women were single mothers and came to exchange views, ideas and problems. Once more their enterprising mindset shone through. As well as their gardening projects they had also been hiring out wedding dresses as most brides would not have been able to afford to buy their own. However their dresses were now so old they could no longer offer them and we discussed how we might get some replacement dresses to them. Subsequently Jackie arranged to take on this responsibility. Bev spoke to the women, explaining how CAFOD wanted to continue to support the Daughters of Charity into the future, but in a way that did not set their expectations too high. One woman, who seemed to be their spokesperson, replied that they appreciated all our help and that our being with them was worth more than money. I was very taken with this reply and highlighted it in my blog.

Later Catherine told me how she had found that when the sisters' translated answers to similar questions, the results were always the much same whoever she asked. This made me think that the comment we had 'heard' through translation might have been too glib to have been accurate. I thought about this a lot. The Sisters were wonderful people, doing incredible good in a completely selfless way – how could I think they were adding their own spin when they translated answers to our questions. I suspect the truth is that they get a number of people visiting their work, all asking similar questions. It must be quite irksome to have a sequence of comparatively wealthy westerners dropping in to ask questions, saying how much help they would like to give and then disappearing. With that in mind I think it's quite understandable that the Sisters do not reflect every nuance in the answers they translate.

We had a lovely Ethiopian meal that evening, eating outside under a blend of starlight and the dim glow provided by the new electricity supply. The room assigned to me was more usually occupied by the team leader Sister Medhin who was often based in Mekelle. Like the cell in Adigrat it was basic but clean and comfortable so I slept well, apart from the cockerel that thought dawn arrived at 2 a.m. Catherine had warned me about him, but that made him no less noisy.

* * * * *

We left Alitena in the Land cruiser just after dawn with a little less room to spare now that Catherine had joined us. My many offers to take my share of being cramped in the back seat were rebuffed by Bev on account of the fact that I had the longest legs. We stopped in Adigrat for some breakfast; when we left we drove along a properly surfaced road for the first time in Tigray.

After about two hours we drove over the summit of a hill and looked down onto the capital city of Tigray, Mekelle. This was where both REST and the Daughters of Charity had their headquarters. We drove into the city, which appeared less polluted and more orderly than Addis Ababa. The roads carried a mix of minibuses, taxis and 4X4's but still there were almost no ordinary private vehicles.

We went first to the Daughters of Charity where we were given a lunch hosted by Sister Medhin. Then Jackie assumed responsibility for Ioan whilst Bev, Catherine and I were driven to REST. We met with Merid, the Deputy Director of REST and another person called

Wereda to review my visit to the Watersheds. I explained how much I had enjoyed the visit and that I had learnt an enormous amount which I would be communicating as widely as possible on my return to the UK. Merid was very positive about my understanding of the project and some of the marketing ideas I had offered.

We talked at some length about what would happen when the current funding expired in 2007, discussing a timetable for new funding submissions that would be presented primarily to the EU. The submission needs to demonstrate how the current project should be consolidated so that the experience gained can be used to promulgate the work to other appropriate parts of Tigray. I asked how a year of real drought might affect the progress made. The REST team was realistic; progress could probably be sustained through a single year of drought but a period in excess of that could reverse a lot of the benefits. One factor was that this had been such a good year for the harvest that there was an understandable tendency to 'make hay while the sun shines' – enjoying the moment while it lasts.

Previous 'exposure visits' like our current trip involving more people from the UK, had been hosted by CAFOD staff and so given a wider but less detailed appreciation of the work. Bev asked which approach REST thought was the most successful. Merid was quick to say that my 'in-depth' visit was more worthwhile, but I expect his involvement in previous trips was limited so he would have had little to compare it with. The other REST staff wanted the best of both worlds; more people and more in depth, but they felt the quantity was more important.

I admit I felt quite guilty having taken 4 days out of Merid's life during which his whole focus was to accompany me on the trip. Doubtless he was able to do a few other jobs in parallel, but the amount of organisation and effort he must have devoted to accommodating me must have been considerable. All he got in return were a few thoughts on marketing, which he had probably heard before. There was of course the wider benefit of increasing awareness in the UK, but this would be of little direct help to him and his team. I offered to keep in contact and to help in developing future marketing plans as well as with the new funding submissions. In practice, the value of this is likely to be very limited for no other reason than that of communication logistics as Merid had no access to email in Adua.

After returning I have sent Merid copies of my photos, the blog and one of my newspaper articles. He wrote back to express his gratitude and I have since sent him a book on developing marketing plans.

I said my farewells to Merid and we left for the Airport, having collected Jackie and Ioan. This was a better journey than the one to Axum. We were on a jet plane and on time.

We returned to the Ghion Hotel where we were due to spend the remainder of the trip. Catherine and I were reunited with Claire, Paul and Seb who had returned to Addis the day before with Seb suffering from a stomach upset. The three of them had been deeply moved by the plight of so many people affected by the flooding in Dire Dawa the previous August. Although they saw all the positive relief work undertaken by CAFOD and other Agencies I perceived that their visit was also quite harrowing. They had some compensation by being able to see a watershed project similar to the one in Adua before they returned to Addis, which left them with a more positive image to take away.

We were all keen to compare notes, but also did not want to dominate the conversation with our own enthusiasm. We had a great evening back at the Lalibella restaurant where we had said farewell exactly a week ago, though it seemed to be much longer. The same waitress looked after us and amazingly she remembered exactly what we had each ordered at our previous visit.

8

The Great Ethiopian Run

Ethiopia is renowned for the quality of its international runners. It has produced some of the worlds greatest distance runners, the most recent of them being Haile Gebresellassie, who is now one of the country's leading businessmen. The 10 Kilometre Great Ethiopian Run began in 1999 and developed into the major national event of the year. Whilst we were in Addis Ababa we frequently saw runners and joggers in training for the event, particularly around the large central area where the former communist President Megistu had held his 'Red Square' type military parades.

Paul and Catherine had been on a couple of short runs before we left Addis for our assignments and were worried about the effect of the altitude. Once they started to get out of breath it was very hard to recover and they were forced to slow right down or even stop for a rest. These early runs gave them the experience to pace themselves very carefully and by the time they started re-training on our return to Addis they were increasingly confident of finishing, but still not so sure how good their times would be.

I had not planned to be part of the race, expecting to walk round the course as a spectator. However, on our first visit to the CAFOD office I had been given my entry T-shirt along with everyone else. I had never run a 10K course and thought it would not be the most sensible idea to start my first one in the heat and altitude of Addis Ababa! So I resolved to walk round and set myself a target time of 2 hours which is half an hour less than the maximum time allowed to qualify for a medal.

On Saturday, the day before the race, we were taken to the University and shopping markets by Daniel where we all made some purchases. In the afternoon we met a group of young photographers who had been trained as part of a CAFOD project to develop new skills. Their photographs formed part of an on-line exhibition illustrating the lives of Ethiopians as part of a drive to increase awareness and form a positive image of the country. They were due to race with us, taking photo's of the race on the way.

We met several people who were signed up for the run. When asked what they expected their time to be, all gave the same answer, "30 minutes." This is less than the time posted by the winner of the ladies' race in previous years. Confidence in their ability to perform well in their national sport was clearly embedded in all participants.

The sound of loudspeakers dominated the Ghion Hotel on the day of the race. Music and announcements filled the air above the increasing background hubbub of the gathering crowds. We met up outside the hotel with Bev and Jannie who gave us our race security instructions. These were that in the event of 'an incident', we should reconvene at the Ghion. If the Ghion was the scene of the 'incident' we should go to the Hilton, assuming it was still there. Plan 'C' was to meet at some coffee bar *en route* to the Airport. I didn't bother with remembering the name as plan 'C' for us on this trip was to 'high-tail' it out of the country!

To be fair the increasing tension with the Union of Islamic Courts who had taken over many parts of neighbouring Somalia, led to fears about terrorist threats to the race. This meant that the security briefing was essential. As always the better prepared one is, the less likely it is that the preparations will be needed. That's how it was in this case.

We walked to the rendezvous point with the rest of the CAFOD/ Trocaire team some way behind the start line. We passed numerous groups singing, dancing, waving and chanting; many of whom were just entering into the spirit of the event. Others, some of whom still felt the Government had stolen the election in 2005, were warming up to use the race as an opportunity to protest. After taking lots of photo's, Paul and Catherine left to get nearer the start, so that as serious runners they wouldn't be hampered by the likes of me. Claire and Seb went to position themselves so they could film the start and finish. Finding myself caught up in the excitement I was becoming increasingly determined not just to finish but to put in a reasonable walking time. I teamed up with Jackie, Bev's friend and child minder, who had had the same thoughts and we decided to stick together to do the best we could.

CAFOD and partners before the run.
Bev and Jannie are third and fourth from the left

Our attention was taken by some loud shrieking and we watched the front runners take off away from the line. This was the traditional false start and I really have no idea how the officials managed to retrieve the renegades. It is quite probable that many just continued. The elite fields started from different points inside the Ghion grounds, so we never got to see them.

The official surge forward commenced. The solid phalanx of green shirted people began to elongate as the front runners sped away. It soon became apparent that being about half way back in the melee meant that, even if we had wanted to run, the crowds around us would have made it impossible. 25,000 people populating a short 10K course was not conducive to racing unless you started very close to the front. Adding to the challenge were the many groups of political protesters who would stop every few hundred metres, form a circle and shout something that sounded like 'THIEF!'

It was therefore not difficult to stay within our preferred steady pace, although after ten minutes I was getting worried that we hadn't passed the 1K sign. It transpired that there wasn't one. More than anything this really boosted our confidence as we were pleasantly surprised by reaching the 2K sign after just over 20 minutes of brisk walking; often jostling past many slower entrants. At this stage I decided there was no chance that I would fail to finish and jointly our thoughts turned to improving upon the 2 hour target.

The atmosphere was tremendous and unique! The combination of the thousands taking part, however badly, in the main event of their national sport; together with many treating it either as an opportunity to protest, or to party, or both made for a strange and frenetic environment. The runners made all the noise and for most of the route the spectators, who were also numerous, stood and watched in silence; a reverse image of the marathons I'd witnessed at home. Only towards the finish did people in the crowd shout encouragement.

Climbing the hill to the 7K marker we had reduced our target time to 1 hour 40 minutes and were by now getting agitated whenever, usually alongside a government building, fellow runners coalesced into a circle and stopped to chant and wave at the crowds. We increased our speed after 7K and with the finish in sight began to feel quite light-headed with elation. I met a lady who was clearly older than me jogging towards us and away from the finish clutching her finishing medal. This made our potential time look a little silly, but she gave me a big smile as I stopped and applauded her when she passed.

My feelings turned to aggravation as yet another protest group decided to form its circle just in front of the finish line itself, meaning we had to thread our way between them and the side barrier, missing Claire and Seb who had been looking out for us. We crossed the finishing line at 10:35 which, considering we didn't start until well after the official time of 09:00 meant that we'd taken about 90 minutes. We were extremely happy with this.

We had all exhausted the small water bottles that had been given to us well before the finish and were ready for more. Enterprising youngsters were selling small bottles priced at one birr each. They still had a lot to learn about market forces as they could easily have charged ten or twenty times that amount!

We were reunited with Claire, Seb and Paul who had completed the race in 52 minutes and with Catherine who clocked 60 minutes before finally meeting up with the rest of the CAFOD team.

Our attitudes to the race had changed during our time in the country. I started out thinking it was an interesting side show that just happened to be taking place whilst we were there. On the day itself I saw it as a showcase for Ethiopia, building on one of their well renowned strengths and it was great to have been a part of it. For Paul and Catherine I expected the run was always going to be the highlight of their trip. However after they had seen the work of CAFOD's partners on their assignments, I sensed that the importance of the run had reduced in their minds, only to be escalated again, quite naturally, on the day itself.

In the afternoon we relaxed and looked at the many photo's that Seb had loaded onto his laptop, together with the video of the race that he'd taken for Yorkshire Television and the one he'd filmed on his trip to Dire Dawa with Claire and Paul.

That evening Bev and Jannie held a party at their house for us and their staff and partners. The office had been through a difficult time as one of their team, Mesfin, had recently died suddenly leaving a wife and young children; it had hit everyone hard. Jannie and Bev had used the run and their party as an opportunity to regenerate some positive team spirit. The office team had obtained sponsorship for their efforts in the run, the proceeds from which were to be used for the benefit of Mesfin's family as there are no state benefits or insurance in Ethiopia to help in such circumstances. The five of us on the trip discussed how we should thank Jannie and Bev for all their efforts in organising our visit. We decided that rather than buying gifts we would add personal donations to Mesfin's fund; a gesture that was well received.

We had two more days in Addis before departing. Some concern was expressed that we would either be bored or feel low due to the anti-climax however I found this time an invaluable buffer between the harsh world of Tigray and the affluence to which we would soon return. On the Monday we visited the National Museum, seeing the remains of 'Lucy', the fossilized hominid discovered in 1974. We walked around the City, watching tiny segments of the lives of so many people; traveling in minibuses, touting for business in their ramshackle shops or welcoming us with glee into their cafes or restaurants. Children often approached us to beg for money or to sell little bags of tissues; we had learnt that the only sensible way to handle this was to ignore it but they had such beautiful faces and attractive smiles that it was hard to turn a blind eye. That evening we indulged ourselves in the natural hot pools of the Hilton Hotel, an affluent oasis in the midst of relative poverty. Any feelings of guilt were, at least in part, assuaged by the relaxing water as it soothed muscles still aching from the run and the city walk.

On the Tuesday we met up with Bev, spending some really worthwhile time taking stock of the trip in some detail. Afterwards we did some preparation for the media work we would undertake on our return. Our last evening was the only one in which we stayed up later than 11pm and even then not much later!

We left for the Airport after breakfast on Wednesday morning and caught the Ethiopian Airways flight home, stopping at Rome *en route*. The whole trip had excited and enthralled each one of us, but now it was time to go home and we were all looking forward to it.

9

The Aftermath of the First Trip

Once back in England I began the media work again in earnest. The day after landing I was up early to appear live on Martyn Coote's '3 Counties' programme in Milton Keynes. More live interviews, this time much longer ones, took place in the studios of BBC Radio Berkshire and BBC Radio Northampton. I sent press releases and then articles to all the local papers, a few of which made their way into print. There was one excellent full page spread in the Reading Chronicle, a copy of which has since found its way to Merid who has shown it to Ngisti and Gidey who were focus of the 'story' I had used in the article.

In the following weeks I gave over 30 talks to a range of audiences, some adult and some juvenile which kept the whole experience very much fresh and alive in my mind. I also decided to raise some retrospective sponsorship for my efforts on the run that I hadn't intended to be part of. With gift aid I generated about £500.

I kept in touch with Bev and Jannie; then since Merid acquired an email link from Adua in early 2007 I've been able to communicate more easily with him too. I continue to follow events in the country avidly and as far as possible keep abreast of developments in the watersheds.

In February 2007, at about the same time I had completed the book 'Ethiopia – A Fleeting Glimpse' I received an email from Bev and Jannie inviting me to return. The twin objectives were; to be part of the 'lessons learnt' review of the watershed project and also to offer support in some new projects which aimed to increase demand for the agricultural produce that was now becoming available thanks to the irrigation projects.

I found it hard to believe that I was to return, but it became more real as the whole cycle of preparation began again. Press releases, pre-visit interviews (the media were all as interested as last time), pre-reading and checking out all my health requirements were a lot easier the second time around.

This time was going to be very different; I would be on my own on the trip and meeting with partners even more than before. I would visit different parts of the country around the city of Dire Dawa and different watersheds in an area of Tigray close to Mekelle, rather than Adua.

I left on the overnight Ethiopia Airways flight on April 29th - alone.

10

Dire Dawa

With a population of about 250,000 Dire Dawa is Ethiopia's second city. It is a one hour flight due east from Addis Ababa and being only 1200 metres above sea-level it 'enjoys' a hotter climate than the capital. It is divided in two by the course of the Dachata River.

On 7th August 2006 the area received more rainfall in a few hours than it normally has in a whole year. There was major flooding; over 300 people were killed and many more displaced from their homes, which in many cases were simply washed away.

In the UK we are not complete strangers to flash floods. However the scale of the Dire Dawa flood was significantly greater than anything that has occurred here, even in recent times. Driving around the area nine months after the event the magnitude of the disaster was still all too clear to see. Wide flood plains, temporary accommodation and displaced boulders were all evidence of what for many people must have been an instant hell.

During the November visit Paul met a man called Kassaye Azmeraw who was standing next to the remains of his shop. Paul found out that he had lost 4 members of his family and 3 close friends as the flood hit his house. Three months on from the flood he was dressed all in black to remember those who perished. He had still not recovered from the broken arm sustained whilst clinging to a nearby tree to save himself from the force of the flood water. Paul had no idea what to say to Kassaye – no words could ever adequately express the extent of sorrow or understanding of his loss. Kassaye had not known what the future would hold for him and was understandably not optimistic. In his position who would be? I was unable to find out any more about Kassaye whilst in Dire Dawa.

After the flood there was an immediate relief effort. Many of the Aid Agencies made appeals and provided emergency food, water and shelter for the victims. Nine months later new accommodation was being built and some was now occupied. The aftermath of the flood demonstrated the work of emergency relief by Government and Aid Agencies working together.

One of the local organisations contributing to the flood relief work was the Haraghe Catholic Secretariat (HCS). HCS is a local church-based organisation operating in eastern Ethiopia. It started work in the mid-1980s to provide basic emergency food supplies during the time of the major drought. Since then it has expanded the content and scope of its work to embrace longer term development activities. These include many of the same functions as those performed by REST in Tigray.

HCS works with a number of members of the Caritas network such as CAFOD, as well as with USAID. Its main projects are in agricultural development, ensuring water sanitation and the development of irrigation systems. HCS also runs projects to improve education and the health of both people and animals.

My host in Dire Dawa was Belayneh Belete from HCS. Belayneh was born in Woter near Dire Dawa. He had been educated in Dire Dawa and appeared very eager to learn about any technique that would help the poorer members of his community.

After a day of acclimatisation in Addis, much of it spent in the company of my old friends Jannie and Bev, I caught Wednesday's dawn flight to Dire Dawa where Belayneh was waiting for me.

We visited Woter and saw the primary school where Belayneh was educated. The school, which was at the edge of the village, had large fertile fields of wet soil surrounding it. We drove around the farmlands and up hills past the terraces which had been constructed as part of the water conservation project. The whole scene was very reminiscent of many I had witnessed during the previous November in Tigray. Many different crops were being grown in this successful conservation project that had matured for over three years; the heavy flooding from the torrential rains nine months earlier had not all dissipated and plenty of water was still available.

Behind the school we met a group of farmers whose Chairman was Mustefa Hafise. Four years ago they could only produce one crop of sorghum each year, with the yield depending entirely on the weather conditions. In a good year they would produce a bumper harvest but their selling price would be low because there was plenty available.

Initially, as part of the water conservation project HCS had helped in the building of wells. Farming groups formed around each of four wells from which water was pumped to irrigate the fields allowing for some crop diversification. New members joined the groups, digging their own smaller wells and supplementing them with water pumped from the larger ones.

Now that the water table had risen enough to make the wells redundant for the time being, they can grow three crops of potatoes each year. The four groups have combined into a legal co-operative, increasing their bargaining power when selling their produce. They have received training on potato production, storage techniques and on on how best to market the crop.

The group has been provided with five different varieties of potato to grow in order to determine the one with greatest market potential. They can now supply the demand from the whole local area and are developing a business plan for the production of high value seed potatoes to be marketed over a much wider area. The main problem the group now faces is that the water table is so high that some of the crop rots before it can be lifted. Despite this unusual problem there were few, if any complaints.

Sitting on the damp ground with Mustefa and about eight others I got a real sense of how their lives have changed in the last few years. Some have corrugated roofs rather than thatch, some also have some livestock. Mustefa summed it up for everyone by saying that they felt they had emerged from a long dark tunnel into the light. The education they had received from HCS had more value to them than any number of University degrees; its impact had been so profound!

With the potato farmers

I was back in Ethiopia and back in the 'field'. There was still the same stunning scenery, the complete lack of background noise and the wonderful people whose enthusiasm for a life so transformed by quite modest investments from people like us was infectious.

* * * * *

The main purpose of my visit to HCS was to look at two small but strategically important projects that CAFOD was funding. The first was a pilot 'demand creation' project for products that could be made from tomatoes. With the combination of fertile soil and increased crop cycles there was a surplus of raw tomatoes after the local demand had been met. The project was working on the creation of 'transformational' tomato products such as paste and sauce which would increase the demand for the crop and so improve the price the farmers could attract for it.

The second project was almost the opposite approach. Demand for milk exceeded the supply available from local farmers. This project was about increasing the milk yield from their cows by producing higher quality forage for use as cattle feed.

In my business life I had spent a lot of time devising marketing and business plans, albeit for computer systems rather than tomatoes. Marketing principles are essentially similar whatever product or service is being promoted. My summary of the key elements of a marketing plan is as follows:

- Have a clear, worthwhile goal.
- Identify the target customers you need to persuade to buy from you in order to achieve the goal.
- Understand clearly what these customers currently think and do; know what you would like them to think and do.
- Be clear about the benefits of your product to these customers.
- Identify what achievement of your goal is worth in revenue and profit. This entails building a simple business model based on a volume and price of product established from a) your customer analysis and b) an assessment of production, supply and promotional costs. This plan will be re-iterated as the assessment of volume and costs becomes more sophisticated during the development phase of the project.
- Work out an effective way of 'talking' to your customers.
- Have clear milestones, measure progress relentlessly and be prepared to flex the plan as necessary. Don't be afraid to abandon the plan if it transpires that the goal is unachievable – but don't give up too easily either!

In talking to Belayneh I discovered that he and a few colleagues had received some good marketing training in recent months, so he understood the key principles of developing a marketing and business plan.

I was even more encouraged when he invited me to sit in on a workshop he had arranged to hold during my time with him. This coincidence led to a fascinating couple of hours. In spite of the conversation being in Amharic I was staggered to hear how many western business expressions have found their way into the language; transformational, paradigm, shelf life, promotion and added value being just a few of them. The conversation was translated in part, but I found I understood the gist of much of the rest.

There was an interesting assortment of people at the workshop. They included a production designer with experience of building business plans, two hotel owners who purchase ingredients for their cooks, government officers with a range of different backgrounds and the 'Chairs' of two women's groups who buy and sell food products within their communities. The discussion was to resolve which transformational tomato products would be most attractive to customers and what price they would be prepared to pay for them. The workshop group concluded that tomato paste and sauce were the most likely candidates as both of these were currently imported in tins.

Producing local versions of these commodities to recipes especially suitable for traditional Ethiopian cooking that were packed and distributed in bottles could displace the imported product and might even attract a price premium. The hotel owners were happy to suggest likely quantities and prices while the production designer was quietly confident he could produce a pilot run that would meet the customers' needs and generate a small profit. Clearly any wider sales would add to the overall profitability.

This was an example of newly enthused and trained 'business' people putting their recently acquired skills into practice. Not for them the arrogance of thinking that they knew better than their customers. That's an attitude that has bedeviled many a western business over recent years.

Even with such a well considered start, things can still go wrong. I encouraged them to produce a 'quick and dirty' business plan that could be used as a model for flexing as real costs and volumes became clearer. I was worried that although their training had been good, their lack of real experience could cause them to stumble over unforeseen pitfalls. Supposing that, due to outside pressures, the hotel owners could not remain as supportive as they were at the moment. Could the costs really be low enough to generate a profit for the small pilot and how would they change as volumes increased? Could volumes increase enough to make the whole project sustainable into the future?

The people involved in this meeting were highly enthusiastic and got straight down to the key issues that needed to be discussed. I really hope their scheme succeeds.

Marketing Workshop – Belayneh is on the left.

One of Belayneh's colleagues took me to meet some tomato farmers. Mesfin introduced me to Ahmed Mussa, the leader of a group of twenty farmers growing tomatoes and potatoes. These crops had replaced their sorghum production about five years previously. He explained that the current tomato crop was not really profitable as supply exceeded demand in the local area and the costs of distribution to a wider area were prohibitive. He was attracted to the demand creation project, realising that paste and sauce could be produced at a time when the tomato price was low, creating products with higher value and a longer shelf life.

From the farmers to the diners in local hotels and restaurants this demand creation project had the potential to influence the lives of many people. Even more than that, its principles could guide the development of parallel business ideas and practices that could be adapted for use in a variety of other markets.

* * * * *

Mesfin took me to a meeting of a group of about fourteen women who gathered each day with their milk produce so that one of them could take it to the market in Dire Dawa. These women were mainly single mothers whose sole source of income was 3 birr for each litre of cows' milk they could sell. They each had up to three or four cows, each of which produced about two litres of milk per day.

Because demand for milk exceeded the available supply, HCS was working on a project in conjunction with the local University to produce higher quality feed for the cows to improve the milk yield; the initial aim was to double the yield to about four litres per cow per day.

It was apparent that although tests had proved the potential of the higher quality fodder, the project had not yet produced any tangible results for the group of 'milk women', who were clearly living at a subsistence level. There was a lot of animated conversation in Amharic; the women were grateful for the efforts being made, but frustrated at the lack of progress so far.

The discussion continued for many minutes as more people joined the group with their own contribution. I was left to my thoughts whilst listening to their real pre-occupation and concern with getting more milk from their cows. Of course this was of the utmost importance to them; to double the yield of their cows could lift their quality of life considerably. They would still be very poor but in less abject poverty than now.

I couldn't help comparing their pre-occupation with a single but life changing topic with the things that we get worked up about; where to go on holiday, what car to buy, finding our journey delayed by road works or about some petty issue at work. I realised how guilty I was of such pre-occupations. I was powerless to say or do anything to help the women, only hoping that the work of HCS and others would address their current pre-occupation and guide them to think of other ideas that would improve their lives and those of their children.

With the milk women

* * * * *

I had been in Dire Dawa for three intense days and two hot and noisy nights. I spent some time with Belayneh, learning about the work of HCS and how his own life had progressed from the school in Woter to a senior role in the organisation.

We found time to visit the ancient town of Harar which is the spiritual capital of Ethiopia's Muslim community and considered by many to be the fourth holiest city after Mecca, Medina and Jerusalem. Many of the people I met on this leg of the trip were Muslim, their inter-faith tolerance and working co-operation being extremely encouraging to witness.

We toured around the bustling town but regrettably the museum was closed and we were too early to witness one of the town's alternative attractions – the nightly feeding of wild dogs by the town's so-called 'hyena man'!

Many people in this area regularly chew 'chat', a crop I saw grown in many places. Chat is a mildly stimulating drug that, unlike cannabis, is legal in Ethiopia. Despite its legal status I was happy to turn down the opportunity to try it! Some people I met were quite concerned about the rapid growth in the use of the drug and one even likened the 'problem' to that of the crack industry in Columbia. I certainly did not see anyone severely affected by chat in the way that we see people in England under the influence of alcohol.

While I was at HCS, Amelle and Jacques from the Secours Catholique France (the French equivalent of CAFOD) were also visiting to review some of the projects they were funding. It was very interesting to talk to them; partly because they were anxious to get home to vote in their Presidential elections on which they had very firm views and partly because of the different way their organisation worked. Amelle was a young employee managing most of their work in Africa; Jacques, who was about my age, was a volunteer with the responsibility for directly managing the organisation's work in Ethiopia.

Along with a number of similar volunteers, Jacques worked about two days each week and visited the country twice every year. This seemed a good and cost effective way of working, assuming it was possible to find the appropriate volunteers prepared to commit a significant amount of time for a long period. I wondered whether the same approach might work for some UK based aid agencies.

We were fed quite well; on one particular occasion we dined at a restaurant run by one of the hotel owners who had been at the marketing workshop. We were also pleased to find a restaurant with a French proprietor who guaranteed we could safely eat her salad as she washed it in bottled water!

After my first almost sleepless night in one of the guest rooms at the top of the HCS building I changed tactic. Abandoning the claustrophobic mosquito net (I'd seen no mosquitos anyway) I took the mattress from the corner bed and slept on it on the floor in the middle of the room under the fan. This also gave me the opportunity to close the window, blocking out the noise of dogs and the occasional passing truck.

What I saw at Dire Dawa encapsulated the full breadth of CAFOD's work.

At the very basic level I saw the devastation caused by the August 2006 flash flood and the efforts being made to re-house those affected so they could begin to rebuild their lives. This work builds on the emergency help provided just after the flood with the longer term provision of food, water and shelter. The twin tasks of emergency relief and investment and re-building to return the *status quo* are complementary, different and equally essential.

Next I saw projects (similar to those in Tigray the previous year) aimed at conserving water, ensuring fresh supplies for drinking and enabling the successful production of a greater range of crops giving people a more assured income. This is longer term aid aimed at helping poor people to improve their own livelihoods in a sustainable manner.

Finally I saw how a very low-cost pilot project will allow people to build their own business skills, identifying and building new markets for their products thus potentially cementing their long-term comfort and well-being. When its success is assured the time will be right for agencies like CAFOD to afford these people the chance to be completely self-sufficient, sustained by their own efforts and spirit of enterprise. They won't have our lifestyle but I suspect they wouldn't want it. They will no longer have a daily struggle to survive and for them, barring catastrophes either natural or man made, poverty will be history.

I left Dire Dawa on the evening flight to Addis, arriving back at the Ghion Hotel at about 10pm on Friday evening more than a little tired, with my mind completely engaged and absorbed by three fascinating days.

I just hoped to have been of help in some small way.

11

Return to Tigray

As well as the four watersheds in Adua, the CAFOD/Christian Aid/ EU funded REST project had developed four others in the woreda of Hintalo Wejerat. This was an area about 20 kilometres from the Tigrayan capital Mekelle, around the small town of Adi Gudum.

The project had officially ended in March 2007 but was continuing on the basis of a 'no-cost extension' using funding that had not been spent during the 3 years of the project life.

Regular project reports were made to the funders, particularly to the European Union as the majority funder. A more formal report had been produced at the halfway point by independent consultants based in Mekelle. This report concluded that the project was 'right on track to accomplish many of the activities envisaged by the contract agreement'. It acknowledged that there had been varying degrees of success in the main project components and that there had been some technical difficulties in the water and sanitation components.

A full post-project review, again conducted by independent consultants, was planned to take place in late 2007 after the end of the no-cost extension.

However CAFOD and REST wanted to conduct their own review before the project ended. This would enable them to capture the key lessons learnt which would inform future work; it would also help in the application for funds to continue the current project by extending the geographical area and building on the market development experiences gained so far.

The review would use the methodology of 'Appreciative Inquiry'. This is a very easy, powerful and positive way to enable change which starts by looking at what works and then at how to make it even better. The approach was first articulated by David Cooperrider and Suresh Srivastva[9] in 1986. A landmark study by Cooperrider interviewed one half of an organisation looking for problems and the other half looking for success. The results differed dramatically between the two groups so that when it was reported back the client did not believe that both sets came from the same organisation. Appreciative Inquiry is about the search for the best in people, their organisations and the relevant world around them.

For CAFOD and REST the aim was to identify the very best outcomes from the work of the watershed project. It was a non-threatening review, encouraging involved staff to show off the best results they had achieved during the previous thre years.

A project team had been formed comprising funders, REST itself and other partners. These other partners included Belayneh Belete from HCS, a lady from Irish Aid, certain community leaders and me.

It had been decided to focus on only four components of the project:

- Agricultural development and marketing. (This had been my assignment.)
- Water development
- Community institutions and community capacity building
- HIV and gender interventions.

Half of the team would go to each of the two sets of four watersheds. Belayneh and I were in the half going to Hintalo Wejerat, focusing on the first two of the above components.

* * * * *

On the Sunday afternoon following my return from Dire Dawa I flew to Mekelle with, amongst others, Jannie who was leading the review and Belayneh. The flight was delayed and we arrived at REST HQ at about 6pm for the initial team meeting. This was a little chaotic as many team members were not present yet others from REST who were not part of the

---

[9] For more see http://www.appreciative-inquiry.org/

team were in attendance. There was some confusion as to how the project was being conducted, how many components were to be reviewed and who was to go to which site. Jannie's patience and diplomacy managed to get everyone back on track before we adjourned, a little weary, to the Abraha Castle Hotel.

Our arrival coincided with a football match being played back home between Chelsea and Arsenal. Many were watching this huddled around one of the limited number of televisions in the town and once again the importance of football (and the English Premiership in particular) to Ethiopian men was very apparent. This match had particular significance as it was Chelsea's last chance to prevent Manchester United from becoming 2007 Premiership champions. They failed, but over the next few days this was a major talking point between many people who knew the result and its consequences but had not actually seen the match.

My first visit to Mekelle the previous November was only a few hours long. This time I was to be there for five days and nights. I was to do quite a lot of walking – usually to the local Comel internet café for posting my blogs. Mekelle has a population of about 140,000 and is relatively clean and vibrant. It is not often visited by tourists but is developing fast and is popular with the National government that is dominated by Tigrayans.

On a hill overlooking the town is the impressive Martyrs Memorial, built to honour Tigrayans who gave their lives in the fight to unseat the Derg. I wondered about the wisdom of spending so much on this memorial when the same money could have been ploughed into economic development projects. A few of us visited the memorial and its associated museum early one morning. It was even more impressive close to, telling the story of the Tigrayan people's struggle against the Derg with a vivid display of pictures and artifacts. It was an impressive tale of how a few activists mobilised the whole community to fight oppression. They succeeded, helped a little by the fall of communism in Russia and Eastern Europe which had been the source of much financial support for the Derg. Tigrayans' pride in this achievement prompted the investment in the memorial.

* * * * *

The following morning we were taken by minibus to the REST Co-ordination office at Adi Gudum where we were met by Tadesse Gebrehiwot and some of his small team. Tadesse performed the equivalent role to that of Merid in Adua and in many ways was a very similar character, although as I was in a group meeting with him there was no opportunity to become as close as I had to Merid in the previous November. The description of the project at Hintalo Wejerat watersheds given by Tadesse was illustrated by numerous wall charts and photographs. The objectives of the work were clearly the same as those described to me by Merid in Adua. The same could not be said about the methods of delivery, largely due to the different profile of the beneficiaries and the different topology of the land. 34,000 people lived in the area in 4,500 households.

During the four days of our review we would become very familiar with Tadesse's office in a building that we would call a shed. We would also get used to the long straight dusty road through the town and the little café where we would have coffee or lunch. Lunch always consisted of a small bowl of meat stew and injeera bread, washed down with a bottle of coke and all served by a strikingly beautiful young waitress who looked out of place in the dirty, tatty room in which the customers ate.

We spent these days driving and walking around the four watersheds, meeting the farmers and their families and seeing how water was conserved and then used for crop irrigation. We met local watershed committees, women's groups and many children. The whole experience was completely engrossing and because this time there were experts asking the questions there was much more information to absorb than there had been in Adua. As we walked we also talked with our fellow reviewers which gave another insight into the lives of local people. Rather than offer the reader another diary account I would like to summarise the experience of these four days by describing the lives of some of the people we met and talked to.

* * * * *

ABDU

One of my fellow reviewers was Abdu Mudesir from Agri Service Ethiopia[10] (ASE). ASE is a voluntary organisation dedicated to improving the lives of poor Ethiopians. Abdu had worked with CAFOD on a number of projects in which they and ASE acted as partners. Abdu understood the methods of water conservation and supply very well and was able to describe the way these were carried out in the watersheds.

---

[10] See http://www.agriserviceethiopia.org/

Unlike Adua the topology here allowed for the construction of check dams across a number of the streams that would be in full flood during the rainy season. At about 2 metres deep these dams hold large amounts of water that can be released slowly to irrigate the farmland at pre-determined times of day, agreed between the watershed committee and the local farmers. Where farmers were upstream of the dams, pumps hired either by the committee or by the farmers were used to supply the irrigation. As we walked the dramatic difference in colour between irrigated and non-irrigated land was clearly visible.

We also saw large numbers of hand dug wells. Some of these were extremely deep and were used for local irrigation where the water was extracted by means of a foot operated treadle pump. Also evident once more were the banks planted with elephant grass to minimize erosion and the use of drip irrigation to certain low level crops such as chillies.

Abdu was always ready to answer my questions patiently and thoroughly. I was beginning to feel that quiet professional dedication was a common feature amongst the more highly qualified Ethiopians who had decided to put their knowledge to good use for the benefit of their own countrymen. It was Abdu's investigation that produced the next story.

Abdu on a check dam

* * * * *

KALAYA

Kalaya is a woman in her forties, living in one of the watershed areas where the topology has allowed the regeneration of a spring similar to the one I saw at the project in Adua. Kalaya farms a small plot of land and owns a few cows.

Before the development of the spring-water supply humans and cattle shared the dirty water, drinking from one stagnant and unreliable source which was exposed to water-borne diseases and contained worms and leeches. People used to filter the water with cotton clothes to try to trap micro-organisms before drinking. The few livestock they owned were often stricken with disease from the water, causing many to die.

Fetching and carrying water was normally a chore carried out by the women. Kalaya was one of many who spent about 5 hours a day collecting from the dirty water source. She told Abdu how one day when the queue was particularly long she had to help another woman to give birth.

This daily fight for the most fundamental source of sustenance completely dominated her life, that of her family and of her neighbours. She and her family suffered from diarrhoea and other water born diseases and were forced to spend much of the little money they had on treatment. The most debilitating factor was the loss of working time while walking to the water source and waiting in the queue, then walking to and waiting for help in the medical clinic.

The new spring with its stand pipes and cattle trough serves 148 households and more than 400 animals, providing access to clean and safe water separately for the livestock and people.

The supply is guarded and controlled by the six members of the water committee (three women and three men). The households each contribute a little of their farmed produce to pay for the guard and one birr per cow per year for upkeep and maintenance.

Since the construction of the spring, Kalaya's family has encountered no water born disease and has much more time to earn some income.

The overflow water from the spring is also available for irrigation to twenty farmers, including Kalaya herself. This enabled her to produce vegetables, generating 600 birr in her first harvest. The family now also eats vegetables, improving their nutrition and resistance to disease. It was clear from talking to Abdu that without the spring Kalaya might not have survived until the time he met her.

* * * * *

GOITUM

Belayneh and I spent quite some time with 27 year-old Goitum Hailuf who lives with his mother of 60 and three brothers of 9, 13 and 22 years old in the village of Hagereselam, 10km from Adi Gudum. His father died in 1992 after which Goitum discontinued his education and started to support his mother by working on the land. His brothers now attend 2nd and 3rd grade in their village school.

Goitum and his family were dependent on 0.75 hectares of rain fed land on which they produced cereals such as wheat, barley and teff in rotation. They could produce only enough for six months of the year, then from each May the entire family was dependent upon food aid and casual labour, often eating only cabbage and cactus.

Goitum's life started to improve when the REST project began in 2004. In the course of the construction of a hand dug well to provide water for drinking, there was an overflow of water directly to his adjacent plot. He began to use it to grow chillies, having purchased seedlings from neighbouring farmers. This opportunistic cultivation provided him with an unexpected income of 1,800 birr from his first harvest. 'This was' he said, 'the first time we had a chance to earn this amount of money in our entire lives'.

Goitum decided not to cultivate cereals anymore and switched to horticultural production. REST staff advised him to use his own open hand dug well for irrigation.

With REST's support, Goitum dug a well 8.8 metres deep. He went on an educational visit to another REST project site in Wukro, eastern Tigray, where he learnt how to irrigate land using a foot operated treadle pump. REST provided him with a treadle pump costing 730 birr on credit over two years.

With the use of the treadle pump he started producing garlic, hot pepper, cabbage and cumin on the family land, initially using seeds provided by the project. From these crops he was able to generate a net income of 7,000 birr from his first season's production and to pay back the loan for the pump within a year.

He then purchased a petrol powered pump for 4,500 birr, again on credit. During this time Goitum was pushing his fellow farmers to follow his approach and took them to his plot to show them how the irrigation system worked. As a result of this he sold his treadle pump to a friend for 600 birr.

The introduction of the motorised pump increased the effective use of his time; renting it out when he didn't need it further increased his income. Renting out the motorised pump at a rate of 30 birr per hour contributed to his total income of 12,000 birr in each of the years 2005 and 2006 which enabled him to pay back the loan for the motorised pump within two years.

Goitum is now able to produce three crops each year comprising spices, chillies, garlic, cumin, red onion, tomato, cabbage and potato.

He sells his produce in Adi Gudum and sometimes in Mekelle. In each of the last three years since 2005 he has generated a net cash income of about 19,000 birr.

Goitum has developed a strong understanding of local markets, deciding where to sell by ascertaining the market price in Mekelle. If the price in Mekelle is sufficiently greater than Adi Gudom to justify the journey he sells there.

In either market, if the price is very low he has access to a post harvest store constructed close to Adi Gudum by REST. He is one of a group of 26 using this store, each having a separate partition with a key for access. The store was a very simple construction of wood and corrugated iron, but it was almost unbelievably cool inside.

Today Goitum has three oxen, a donkey, three cows and two calves. He has improved his small living hut with a corrugated iron sheet roof; all family members have extra clothing and are able to eat three times a day. He has been able to save 27,000 birr at the local bank and has over 10,000 birr cash in hand; some of which he loans to other local farmers. Moreover, he has planted eight guava trees, three avocado trees, nine sweet orange trees and seven mango trees, all of which will all begin to bear fruit in two years.

Goitum is a larger than life character, full of ideas and with lots of energy. He proudly showed us records of his bank deposits and the loan agreements he had made with his fellow farmers. At our inaugural meeting with the local watershed committee (of which he is a member), it was apparent that he was a very popular figure and was immediately proposed by his neighbours as their best example of someone who had seized with great zeal the new opportunities offered to him.

Goitum's story is one of rags to relative riches, initiated by the REST project but achieved by his own ingenuity and instinctive entrepreneurial skill. It is an inspiring story – I called Goitum 'The Apprentice' in my blog, as a reference to the BBC television programme hosted by Sir Alan Sugar.

GOITUM and his mother

* * * * *

GEBREKIROS

I met Gebrekiros Kelelew who used to farm a small area of land which produced a meagre crop of sorghum. To enhance this income he also ran a small tea shop but still could not afford to send his children to school. Gebrekiros is a quietly spoken man, tall and with the rugged features I had become used to seeing on the faces of so many Ethiopians in their middle age.

Three years ago Gebrekiros was selected by the Watershed Committee to receive one of 10 available 'exotic' cows from another part of Ethiopia. These cows have a better milk yield than the local breed so he obtained a 5 year credit agreement for 4,500 birr to pay for the cow.

This animal now produces twenty litres of milk per day which he sells via the local milk co-operative for 3 birr per litre giving him a gross monthly income of 1,800 birr. The co-operative has thirty member farmers who share the work of running it in turn; each giving about one day of his time every month to serve as a cashier. The co-operative has developed an acute sensitivity to the market. It turns about half the milk into butter and sells its products primarily in Adi Gudum but also in Mekelle. They also arrange to transport the product further afield during the local Christian fasting periods when, for about 70 days per year, milk products are not consumed. They go to Muslim areas like Afar, where although they make less money because of transport costs, they are at least able to obtain income from their supply during these periods.

The cow has since produced a 2-year old bull and twin young calves (one of which is also a bull). Gebrekiros will sell the bulls at their most profitable age and will use the young cow to produce more milk once it is old enough.

Gebrekiros was able to send his children to school once he had started to gain income from the cow. His son has just received his 10th Grade diploma and his 19 year old daughter is at Computer school in Mekelle. Her fees and local accommodation cost him about 300 birr per month. He now uses his small plot of land to produce fodder for the cows, has built an extra room onto his house and has abandoned his tea shop!

He and his wife now have a much more comfortable life and he feels he has given his children the best start in life that he could.

Gebrekiros and his wife

* * * * *

GIRMAYA

While I was with Gebrekiros, Belayneh was meeting Girmaya Kidanu who lives in the village of Maye-deru 22 km south-west of Adi Gudem. Girmaya is a 30 year old married man with one daughter. Unlike most farmers in the area he owns no land and was forced to depend on daily casual work since he married four years ago. Prior to his marriage he was living with his poor parents on less than half a hectare of land. When there were no casual jobs available in his village he would walk to Adi Gudem or Mekelle to find work.

He was not impressed by the arrival of the REST water conservation project as he had no land to irrigate, so at first he was reluctant to be part of the community meetings organised to discuss the project with the local villagers. He was, however, able to benefit from providing his labour in the construction phase of the project

As previously degraded land was reclaimed by the construction, twenty six landless people including Girmaya were each provided with 2,500 square metres of land to manage. After being trained in beekeeping they were each provided with modern beehives and accessories on credit. The loan was 600 birr and had a five year repayment period. The group of twenty six has now become a legal co-operative, working together to develop the beekeeping business.

In his first year of production, Girmaya was able to harvest 30 kg of honey selling each for 35 birr. He then acquired a second hive on credit producing 60Kg of honey in one season giving a total income of 2,100 birr per season and over 4,000 birr per year. Honey is in great demand so Girmaya and his colleagues can easily sell all they produce.

Girmaya has improved his house by adding a corrugated iron roof and can now feed his family from his own efforts, not needing to resort to casual labour. He plans to acquire more hives and the co-operative aims to open a shop in the village to sell honey and other goods.

* * * * *

There were many other stories. Simret, who is now a woman member of the Watershed Committee, used to earn her living in the sex trade. The project trained her in weaving and provided her with a hand loom. Simret now earns 3,600 birr each year, is able to send her three young children to school and has bought herself a donkey.

One afternoon I was walking with Tadesse through the town, watching the various markets at work. We visited a small technical co-operative which produced windows and doors, as well as gates for the check dams. Their income arises both from the local people and from Government whose main contribution is in the form of goods such as tools, electricity and the building they work from.

We saw the building that was being refurbished so that it could become the new location for the milk co-operative of which Gebrekiros was a member. It was in a much better location, although to my eye it didn't seem to offer much more in the way of space, facilities and comfort than the one they were to leave.

By the time Thursday, the fourth day, was well underway I began to feel that I was overloaded with 'good news' stories. This, of course, was the objective of the review, but I felt increasingly that I wanted to see for myself what life really was like for people who had not enjoyed the benefit of the interventions created by the REST project. This was not going to be possible as the nearest I had come to seeing people who really were living in poverty was in meeting the milk women in Dire Dawa. What I did want to do, however, was to try to discover how many Ethiopians were still living the sort of life that Goitum, Gebrekiros, Kalaya and Girmaya had lived before their respective worlds were changed.

That Thursday afternoon after Jannie had returned from his part of the review in Adua we both paid a visit to the Daughters of Charity. They were as lively, positive, generous and full of ideas as they had been the previous November. I gave Sister Medhin twenty football shirts for the Mekelle street children. These had been donated by a school in Nottingham and formed part of a batch that would be given to the children when the remainder arrived with another CAFOD volunteer during the summer. I emailed Catherine a photo of the Sisters to which she replied saying that it had brought a large lump to her throat!

12

Watershed Review Presentation

The next day we all walked from the Hotel to REST HQ, fully prepared for a busy and illuminating morning giving feedback on our own experiences over the previous four days and listening to others.

Soon after my arrival I found Merid talking to some of his colleagues in an office adjacent to the conference room where we were due to meet. He broke off to give me a very warm Ethiopian style welcome; a firm crash of right hands and shoulders. Merid had been hoping that I would be part of the Adua review team. It would have been very interesting to return to the locations of my first visit to see how things had changed; however, visiting the parallel project and meeting a whole range of different people had provided a different viewpoint. Merid looked really well and was now the proud owner of a mobile phone although it had the weirdest ring tone; one which was often to be heard as he was now clearly quite dependent upon it.

I gave Merid a copy of my book 'Ethiopia – A Fleeting Glimpse', a book on Marketing principles he had asked for and a small game for his boys. We didn't have much time to chat before the presentation, but he came in the car with me to the airport afterwards and gave me an update on the progress of his projects.

About twenty people listened to the presentation, almost all of whom were senior staff from REST. The Adi Gudum team, which had covered agricultural production, marketing and water development, presented first. Belayneh talked about Goitum, Abdu gave an account of the water conservation activities and told the story of Kalaya, amongst others, whilst I talked about Gebekiros. There was a lot of discussion as to why these people had been so much more successful than others and what could be done in the future to replicate their achievements. I felt that the biggest factor was the character of the individuals; many were inspired by the chance to improve themselves and just couldn't help advancing further. Others were happy to accept their improved circumstances and didn't feel the urge to make additional progress. The general view of the Ethiopians present was that the younger and more religiously minded people were those who benefited most and were also more enthusiastic about ensuring their new skills and good fortune were exploited to the full.

The Adua team had covered community institutions and community capacity building, together with HIV and gender interventions.

More committees than I would have expected had been formed to oversee the work of the projects, probably because the remnants of the controlling culture of the former communist regime were still present. However they did seem to work.

In all parts of the project the key driving force was the Watershed Committee, always with a strong Chairman who was a very good communicator. There were sub-committees on topics such as water and sanitation which would oversee the development and management of these facilities, making decisions as to who were the best people to benefit from them. Members of all Committees were elected by the community, with REST staff ensuring fair play.

There were also Associations and Cooperatives overseeing, for example, financial management or marketing of commodities such as milk and honey. There were also user groups comprising local people who would feed back information on facilities such as water pumps to ensure they were used fairly, were protected and that any problems were brought to the attention of the Watershed Committee. Finally at every watershed there was a specific Women's Group whose task was to oversee the improvement of women's participation in local activities. Women often act as traders, buying and selling small items within their local village, giving them some small additional income to supplement their income from farming activities.

We heard how in one Adua watershed there was a determination by the local people to ensure that their representatives on the committees were all young people. There was a willingness to accept leadership by the young, an attitude particularly encouraged by the religious leaders who have considerable influence in the communities. At the same watershed the children were encouraged to save any small amounts of money they were given or had earned; the objective being to give them an early insight into the financial world and to enable them to have a small amount of cash in hand when they were ready to begin their own working lives. There were some in the meeting who felt this was inappropriate; that children should concentrate on their education and not on building up cash but this was a minority view.

We hear a lot about 'community cohesion' here in the UK. In Tigray it is taken for granted. Born out of real hardship, the need to work together has now developed into a determination to share the benefits of new found fortune. Whenever I found myself sitting in a Committee or Co-operative I was impressed by the businesslike and good homoured way they conducted their conversations.

The final presentation was given by Feven Tadesse, a female colleague of Merid; her subject was gender and HIV. There are numerous projects in Ethiopia to cleanse and improve water supplies, improving health and livelihood opportunities for the beneficiaries. In parallel the REST projects also addressed social challenges typified by the perceived need of the funders to change the historic subservience of women and to address the growing HIV/Aids crisis. Although the initial impetus for emphasising social issues came from the NGO funders and to a lesser extent the Government, it was noticeable that local staff of organisations such as HCS and REST had also become fully convinced of the benefits of this focus.

With an eloquence and sparkle worthy of a seasoned TV presenter, Feven told us a number of stories.

Wahid is 15 years old, with two elder sisters and two younger brothers. At home all menial tasks were handled by her mother and the three girls while the father controlled all the finances; often borrowing money without consulting the rest of his family. He also selected husbands for both of Wahid's elder sisters. Wahid joined a 'gender' club that was sponsored by the project and held in her school giving her an insight into the problems the family was facing as a result of her father's behaviour.

She wanted to see her family change and discussed with her mother what she had learnt from the club. The project commenced a programme of training for whole families and her Father was persuaded to join in. He began to see that the family's life could improve if he played a greater part in their daily routine. Wahid told Feven of the day when her youngest brother started crying whilst her mother was out of their house doing another chore. In the past her father would have ignored the crying child, but on this occasion he picked him up and comforted the boy. This simple act told Wahid that things were changing; her family is now a much closer unit, sharing the workload and discussing future plans together.

Atsede is thirty seven, married with one son and one daughter who attend the senior school in Adua, some way from their home. Highly respected in her village, Atsede could not read and was dependent on her husband or neighbours for reading documents or letters from relatives. When the project set up an adult literacy programme Atsede was the first to register. Three years later, with the course completed, Atsede has been able to join the local watershed committee to fulfil both her ambition and the wishes of her local community supporters. She is now participating in a training programme that will enable her to pass on her literacy skills to others and is determined that her age will never limit her desire to pursue her education.

Gebrehaweria is 16. He lives with his parents and attends High School in Adua where he has joined the HIV/AIDS Club at his school. He now realises that he had many misconceptions about the virus, assuming it could only be transmitted by sexual intercourse. The Club members were given awareness training by the project which taught them about the risks of using shared blades for shaving and nail cutting. He started to talk to his family about the threat that the virus posed to them all.

His elder brother was about to become engaged so Gebrehaweria persuaded him to take a blood test with his fiancée before the wedding; which they did and happily both were clear. He also has a married sister whose husband is very mobile in his search for work. Gebrehaweria shyly but firmly advised him to be faithful to his wife for the sake of both of them and their children. Gebrehaweria told him if he wasn't faithful then he should take a blood test before sleeping with his wife again. This was not an easy thing for Gebrehaweria to do, but his conscience is now clear, having warned of the potential risks to his family members who might not have been aware of them.

I was very moved by Feven's presentation and whenever I was asked which was the best presentation of the meeting I always replied that it was hers.

Feven giving her presentation

The whole discussion at the meeting was very positive, as expected by the nature of the review. It was not the time or place to identify whether better results could have been achieved or if there might have been more efficient methods of utilizing donors' funds. These things will emerge later in the year in the formal post project review which I hope I will see.

So what were the lessons learnt? At the most basic level it is obvious that water means everything. Without water it is impossible to survive;

with it the opportunities people have are almost boundless. We didn't need a review to tell us that, but what did emerge were examples of the ingenuity with which many beneficiaries used their new found supply to develop economic and social activities that bettered themselves, their families and their neighbours. There were many ideas that could be fed into future work to stimulate more people, lifting them out of poverty in the future.

However for me the real benefit was the sharing of knowledge between the review participants. As an example Belayneh spent ages inspecting the vegetable store near Adi Gudum which was of a completely different design to those I had seen used by the potato farmers near Dire Dawa. He was keen to understand the benefits that this design gave to the storage process so that he could inform his HCS colleagues.

On the way to the airport for the return flight to Addis, Merid gave me an update on his Adua projects . The spring at the St Michael watershed on which so much local development was based still flowed well, nine months after the rains. This was doubly pleasing as it was also the background to most of my talks back home.

Merid had been able to find enough money to buy more gabion to improve the conservation of water at the Tsigereda watershed. At Tsigereda the metalworking bakers were thriving and had widened their market by offering a 'drive through' service on the main road out of Adua. I told him how concerned my audiences in the UK had been when they saw the bare wires that supplied their home-made oven with electricity and suggested that maybe we should now buy them a proper switch!

It was a shame that I had so little time with Merid, but we resolved to keep in touch via his new internet connection at Adua, although when he described it to me it was apparent that its reliability left something to be desired.

We arrived back in Addis at about 7pm – I was ready for an early night – but Jannie informed me that Bev was taking me out for dinner.

13

Addis Ababa

At the start, middle and end of the trip I spent a total of five nights at the now familiar Ghion Hotel. My time in Addis was well filled, usually by arrangement with Jannie and Bev. I did have a little time to myself and felt quite comfortable walking around the area close to the Hotel and in Meskel Square. On a couple of occasions I was approached by someone claiming to be an off-duty member of the hotel staff, offering to take me to see a 'cultural event laid on for foreign tourists'. This is an easy scam to walk away from and I'm told that if I had accepted I would have come to no harm but my pocket would have been a lot lighter; an exorbitant charge would have been made for a pretty poor piece of entertainment.

I often went to the Hotel gardens which were regularly used by wedding parties who stopped there for photo shots *en route* to the wedding breakfast. At any one time there might be up to a dozen parties scattered around the grounds, with stunning brides and their many 'intimate friends' in a variety of colourful costumes. The wedding parties often blocked the road leading to the Hotel meaning that when heading for the airport to fly to Mekelle I had to run down to the main road, complete with luggage ready to leap into Jannie's car before the local police noticed that he had stopped where he shouldn't have.

Bev and Jannie looked after me well. They took me to a brunch party with a number of other western families, entertained me on three occasions at their house, the scene of the post race party on the first trip and they took me to lunch at a nice western-style restaurant after a guided tour of the city. At their house one evening we were joined by Julian Filochowski, the former CAFOD Director, who was in town on an assignment for another Aid Agency. It was fascinating to hear how Julian had helped the Charity grow from an income of less than £2m per year to over £25m in a period of twenty years. Julian's knowledge of the developing world was enormous; he clearly had affection for Ethiopia having initially visited during the 1985 famine with Cardinal Basil Hume.

That final Friday after returning from Mekelle, Bev took me to a dinner with the Ethiopian Catholic Secretariat. Each Diocese has a Secretariat, HCS being the one for the Haraghe Diocese, based in Dire Dawa. They had just finished their annual meeting, of which Bev had been a part. Other members of Caritas International were present along with Diocesan representatives. This was a very informal affair (I'm pleased to say), made even more so by the loud music which prevented all but the most stentorian attempt at conversation.

The city seemed busier than on my first trip with more traffic jams and a lot more construction work, much of which was in preparation for the Millennium celebrations in September 2007. Although not as appealing as many cities in Western Europe, I had grown quite attached to its unique atmosphere – crowded yet safe, busy yet relatively quiet. Jannie drove me through it for the last time the day after we returned from Mekelle, delivering me to the highly fortified airport for the night flight home.

14

Afterthoughts

There are many experts on Ethiopia, its history, economy, politics and people. All I can offer are a few observations from someone with no background of the country who simply observed what he saw in two fleeting visits. Cynics might say I was only shown what CAFOD had pre-determined would give me a positive view. Of course they wouldn't send me somewhere that would give a bad impression, but I was let loose into local organisations with only local people to talk to, albeit often through the local contact acting as interpreter. However, I also kept my eyes open and many of my afterthoughts are built on simply watching people getting on with their lives.

AID

'Does our money really help?' In Ethiopia I saw nothing that would suggest any money gets siphoned off in an inappropriate way. After the 18% taken for CAFOD's education, fund-raising and governance expenditure the rest is allocated to international projects. In managing these there is the cost of the country operation in Addis Ababa. I was struck by Bev and Jannie's attitude towards keeping their costs as low as possible and not succumbing to the invasive infection called 'mission creep' and its inevitable additional costs. Their role is to ensure the partners perform as efficiently and effectively as possible. Using well known partners on the ground is a much more cost effective approach than employing more in-country staff to conduct the projects. Partners' staff were more experienced and better able to ensure the smooth running of projects than any locally hired direct staff could be, unless they were recruited from potential partners anyway. In Adua, Merid worked very hard, including most weekends and I saw plenty of evidence of real commitment from his team. However some of the project funding would have been used legitimately to fund the REST HQ overhead.

It should be remembered that it is not just CAFOD and Trocaire money that the local office is managing, but also that of other donors who, as a result of the office's reputation for professionalism, have entrusted them to oversee their own contributions to local projects. 90% of the watershed funding did not come from CAFOD or Trocaire, but from Christian Aid (10%) and the European Union (80%).

It is hard to draw a line between the element of spend that is management overhead within Ethiopia both within CAFOD / TROCAIRE and REST and that which is directly spent on expertise and materials for the projects themselves. I would argue that without an element of strong management, for which there is a cost, spending on expertise and materials would be less controlled and therefore less effective.

In the worst case let us assume that a 10% overhead expenditure services the internal management needs of the in-country and partner organisations and is not directly involved in overseeing project work. (This represents 5% for each organisation – a figure that many would recognise as legitimate.) This would reduce the 82% of donations currently channeled to projects down to 72%. This would mean that 72% of our donations directly benefit poor people and the other 28% is invested for the future in education and campaigning to ensure increasing donations and effective use of the existing funds. To my mind this is still a great return on our money. The 28% is also covered by the gift aid contribution from the Government which is payable on the majority of donations to CAFOD.

The effective buying power of £1 in Ethiopia is about ten times that in the UK. The benefit in terms of lives saved and lives transformed adds another multiplier which is impossible to quantify. So let's keep donating with enthusiasm and generosity.

Inter-government aid is a different matter and one on which many are better qualified to pass judgment than I am. However my perception is that it is certainly more bureaucratic and conditional, it carries more overhead and is therefore much less effective and controlled than aid through NGOs. I understand that the British Government and others want to move towards forms of 'direct budget support' where more money goes directly to government's poverty reduction programmes and less into overheads.

I talked to a number of people about how many Ethiopians still had no close access to clean water. It was hard to obtain a definitive answer, but my assessment is that about 30% of the population has clean water on tap within about twenty minute's walk of their homes. The latest UN figure is 22%[11]. Twenty years ago this figure would have been less than 1% so real progress has been made by the Government and Aid Agencies. Even so, about 70% of Ethiopians still have their lives dominated by searching and queuing for that which we in the west take for granted.

ERITREA

The conflict with Eritrea brought me to despair. Here are two peoples as culturally close as those between adjacent Counties in England who had seemed reconciled after Eritrea had won its independence. After the subsequent conflict in which many tens of thousands of lives were lost on both sides (I got several different estimates of precisely how many died) there is now a complete stand-off with a high level of border tension that could flare up again at any time. With so many families on each side affected by the war, the level of suspicion and hate is incredibly high for two nations that should be very close and would have so much to gain from peace.

Eritrea's size must mean that its economy would benefit from trade with Ethiopia, which in turn would benefit from the reopening of its closest routes to the coast. If the huge amounts of money currently being spent by the respective militaries were ploughed back into infrastructure investment it would make a world of difference. It's so completely exasperating. Like so many disputes that seem absurd to the outsider, when you are inside them they seem intractable. If you want to get really depressed then you should read the propaganda each Government issues

---

[11] UN figures given at http://www.irinnews.org/country.aspx?CountryCode=ET&Region Code=HOA

about the other![12] The best hope is that eventually the protagonists will realise that the economic cost is too great for the conflict to continue. When this happens it is to be hoped that someone or some suitable body will step in to broker a lasting peace.

ECONOMY

The economy is growing well although the future is not without its challenges.

One of these challenges is to obtain a just reward for 15 million Ethiopians reliant on the coffee trade. Coffee is Ethiopia's largest exported crop comprising 90% of the total and representing 54% of GDP. It is grown by traditional methods but does not command the premium it should as the growers don't have the expertise or resources to pass the stringent tests for organic definition.

During my first visit the Chief Executive of Starbucks was visiting Ethiopia's Prime Minister Meles Zenawi to discuss a trademark dispute that many claimed was depriving Ethiopian growers of substantial revenue. This is a complex issue, but the simple fact is that a tiny increase in the price that coffee buyers pay to growers will have a dramatic effect on the income of Ethiopians dependent on this trade.

It underlines the premise that real escape from poverty comes not just by increasing aid but from setting trade rules that are not weighted in favour of the rich and I was pleased that the particular dispute with Starbucks was resolved before my return trip. However, it is a sobering thought that for each cup of coffee drunk in one of the many outlets we now have in the UK (Starbucks, Costa Coffee, Café Nero, Coffee Republic etc), little more than a few pence of the £2 purchase price will find its way back to coffee growers in Ethiopia or any other developing country. If we paid a few pennies more we could double their income.

This is typical of the whole trade imbalance issue that is addressed by the Fairtrade Foundation. It is also vividly portrayed in a newly released film called Black Gold[13].

---

[12] The Ethiopian view summarised in various statements to his parliament by Meles Zenawi. This is at http://www.ethioembassy.org.uk/news/news.htm

Eritrea's views are spelt out on its web site http://www.shabait.com/staging/index.html

[13] See http://www.blackgoldmovie.com/

The transport infrastructure is hindering potential growth in tourism. Lalibella and Axum would have great appeal to many more western tourists interested in history and archeology. The air links are there but the road infrastructure is very weak. The dichotomy is that any investment to improve the infrastructure would take time, during which the awareness of the climatic impact of transport could reduce the numbers willing to travel.

In Tigray, local production often exceeds local demand so farmers and growers are looking for new markets. The entrepreneurial spirit is strong but here again the infrastructure and potential transport costs could limit the success of some of the many bright marketing initiatives that will certainly be made.

We put forward many ideas during the first visit, including the creation of a spiritual retreat market built around the Faithful spending time with the Daughters of Charity. We got quite excited about this prospect, as did the Sisters until we remembered the FCO advice about not going near the Eritrean border!

The investment in a mobile phone network could open up opportunities for internet based businesses even in remote village areas if the line charges were not prohibitive. With increasing education for a fast growing population, breaking out from the dominance of farming will be vital to ensure employment for the time when today's children become adults.

Ultimately the children's keenness to learn, the determination of many to break out of poverty by their own efforts and the continuing catalyst of development aid gives me great hope for the economic future of the country. The main restraint could well turn out to be regional conflict.

POLITICS

The residue from the post-2005 election protests still exists. The truth about the protests is probably somewhere between the Government's view of an armed insurrection that needed to be quelled and the protestors' view that police fired on unarmed demonstrators. In a recent interview with Jonathon Dimbleby[14] Prime Minister Meles

---

[14] The Jonathon Dimbleby interview with Meles Zenawi was broadcast in June 2007 on Teachers TV

Zenawi asserted his commitment to democracy and also indicated that he would be standing down before the next election. Meles was the very first Ethiopian leader to introduce a democratic voting system; he said he was sorry the police reacted in the way they did, but insists that there had been a real attempt to overturn a legitimate election result by force. During the period of my visits there was no evident unrest and the Government appeared to be in control.

A number of opposition party members had been tried for attempting to overthrow the Government, found guilty and sentenced to life imprisonment. They asked for pardon which has been granted and they have been freed, still protesting their innocence and remaining publicly critical of the Government. How they behave in the future and how the Government responds to any further criticism will be an indication of how stable the country really is.

Meanwhile the economy continues to grow well at about 10% each year and Meles Zenawi proudly boasts that 13% of GNP is being spent on education. This is a very high figure, although to be fair I saw a lot of evidence of considerable investment in education. Having seen the history of the struggle by Zenawi and his party represented at the Mekelle Museum, I can understand his reluctance to give up hard won power.

PEOPLE

There were stark differences between the way of life of Ethiopians and our own in the UK as will have been apparent from my earlier descriptions. In my view the major differences are in the much stronger community cohesion and tighter family ties that exist in Tigray and Dire Dawa. People pull together, the old and sick are cared for within the family, crime rates are low and everyone appears happier. They would simply not understand our way of life or survive in it, any more than we could tolerate theirs. We are scandalously profligate and hugely affluent; they are poorer than they deserve to be. The answer is for us to skim a little of our riches off the top and transfer them to the third world, not as aid but as support and encouragement.

The Government should be given credit for its anti-corruption campaign, but it will take time to permeate down to all levels. We found many examples of the old communist-inspired attitudes of central control, bureaucracy and the overbearing treatment of customers. In one instance Seb nearly tore his hair out over the import and export procedures for his photographic equipment. There were also some notable exceptions when our expectations were exceeded. I remember an elderly male receptionist at the Ghion on the first visit who always handed us the right room keys as we approached the desk without having to be reminded of our room numbers!

MY QUESTIONS

Finally, let me return to the opening questions, about which there has been much written by others, to make an 'outsider's' comments based on my short exposure to one challenged African nation.

Is the government siphoning off money destined to help their people?

I saw no evidence at all that any money donated to the Aid Agencies gets anywhere near national or local government. On the contrary, government officials that I met were very supportive of all the work conducted by local NGOs and in many cases added value to their efforts by ensuring they dovetailed into any government investments, particularly in the field of education.

Have people have become too dependent on outside help, and has it dampened their motivation to help themselves?

I'm sure it must be apparent from everything I have written that I met nobody who seemed to believe that their livelihood was owed to them by charity. There was frustration in the minds of the milk women of Dire Dawa, but this was because so far, efforts to help them had not been successful. I'm sure there are lazy Ethiopians, but everyone I met was keen to be responsible for their own future. They appreciated the help we offer but did not want to become dependent on it.

Is there too much money spent on conflict and strife between and within countries rather than on developing health, education and economic growth?

Undoubtedly! In his Jonathon Dimbleby interview, Meles Zenawi claimed that Ethiopia's defence budget was 2% of GDP – a figure that seems too low when the troop levels in Somalia and on the Eritrean border are considered. Of course this money could be better spent, although the need for defence and security is paramount for any country, particularly one with Ethiopia's turbulent background of resisting all serious attempts at colonisation.

Are the trade rules as defined by the rich Countries, harming the development of businesses in Africa's poorer nations?

Again the answer is a resounding "Yes!" There must be a continuing unremitting campaign by Aid Agencies and wherever possible by governments to ensure that the rules imposed by rich countries do not prejudice the prospects of poor nations.

My final lay judgment is that there are two key parameters that will lift Ethiopia and other poor countries out of their relative poverty. These two are; economic growth stimulated by fairer trade rules and education. Continuing support from relatively small amounts of targeted help given by rich donors will help improve living conditions so that beneficiaries can concentrate their efforts on those two key parameters rather than on a struggle to survive.

Back home it was disturbingly easy to slip back into the old routine. The trips were life changing experiences in that they made me appreciate just how much we have in our western lives; things that are not absolutely essential, but which we have come to treat as if they are. I also hope that I am a little more patient and somewhat less pre-occupied with the trivial problems that occur from time to time.

A few vivid memories stand out and it is these that are constant reminders both of how much we have to be grateful for and of what, due to our prosperity, we have lost from our lives.

- With no cars, televisions or computer games, the Ethiopian village world is silent except for the sounds of nature.
- The worries of the poor are real concerns; think of the milk women in Dire Dawa compared with our agitation over quite unimportant inconveniences in life.
- The unbounded enthusiasm of poor people upon seeing the change in their fortunes made possible by our small donations is quite uplifting.

The big wide world is a complicated, unstable and frenetic place. There is little that we as individuals can do to affect global conflicts, natural disasters or the meanness of spirit displayed by some of our fellow men.

What we can do is to help. Painlessly and inexpensively we can help to change the lives of some of our fellow citizens who, through no fault of their own, have not had the same chances in life as ourselves.

Yes, our money really helps!

www.ingramcontent.com/pod-product-compliance
Lightning Source LLC
Chambersburg PA
CBHW031231280526
45784CB00004B/1525